CHRISTIAN MUSICIAN

Christmas Worship

ISBN 0-634-06246-8

HAL•LEONARD®
CORPORATION
7777 W. BLUEMOUND RD. P.O. BOX 13819 MILWAUKEE, WI 53213

Visit Hal Leonard Online at
www.halleonard.com

CONTENTS

ANGELS MEDLEY

Arranged by TIM AKERS, CHARLIE PEACOCK,
MICHAEL PASSONS, JANNA POTTER,
NIKKI HASSMAN and JODY McBRAYER

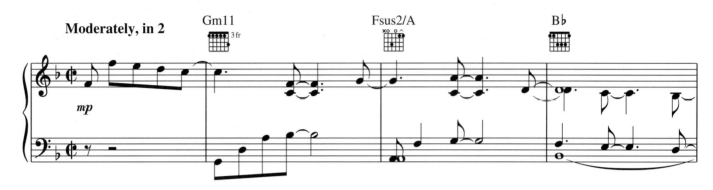

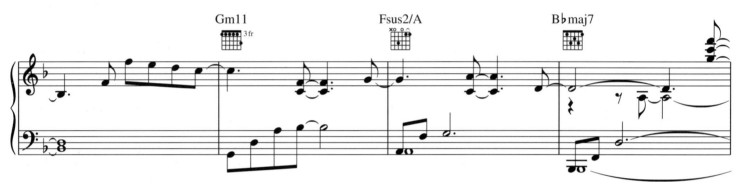

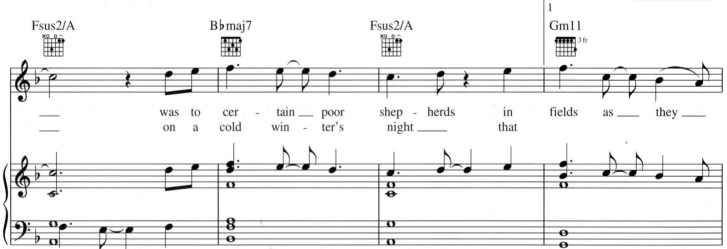

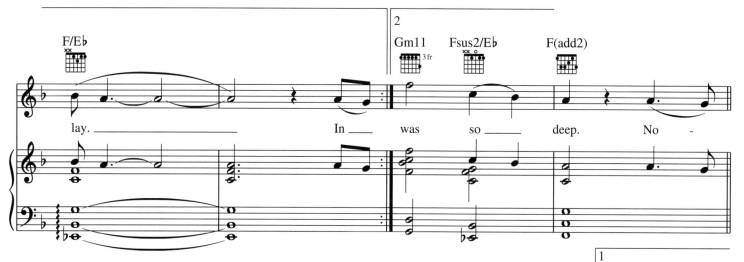

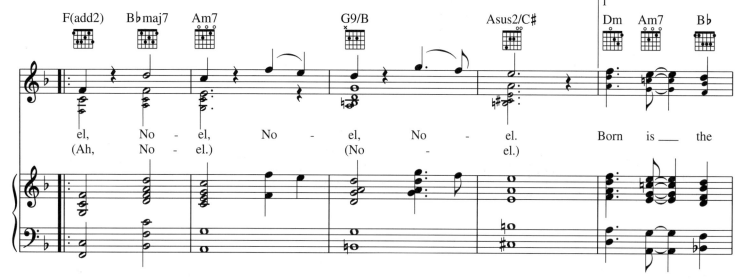

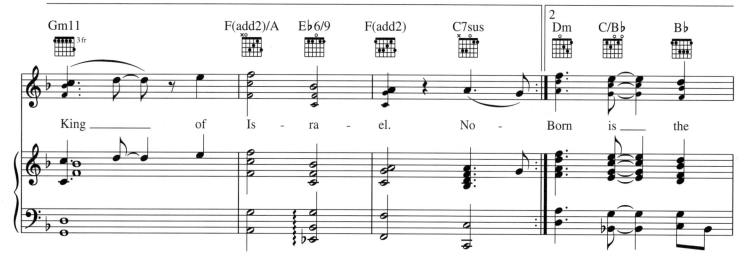

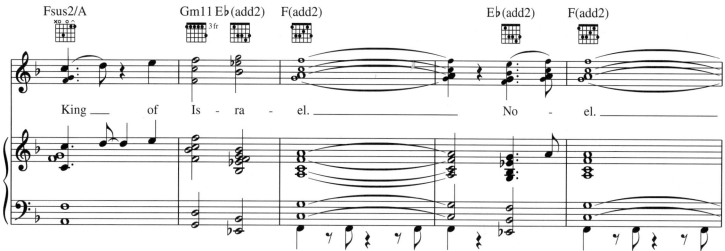

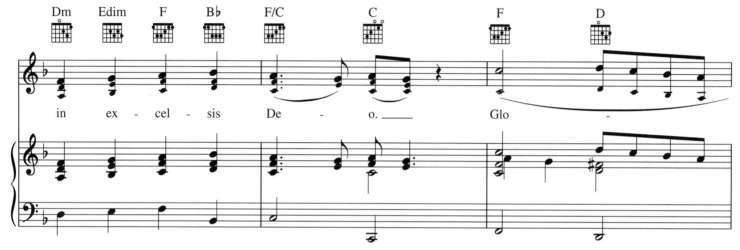

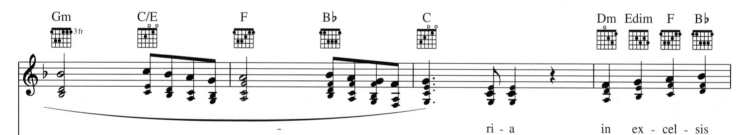

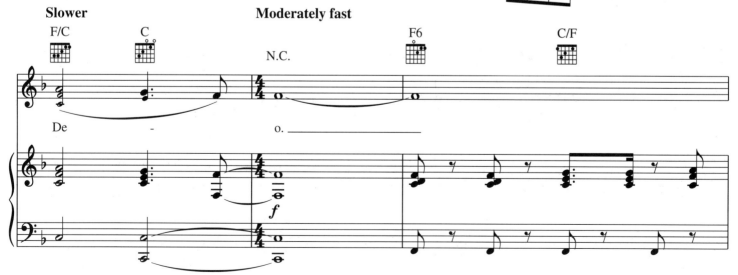

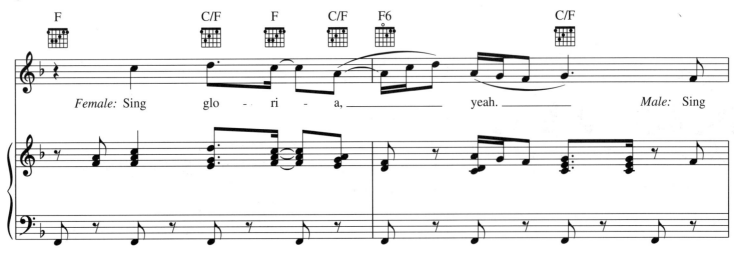

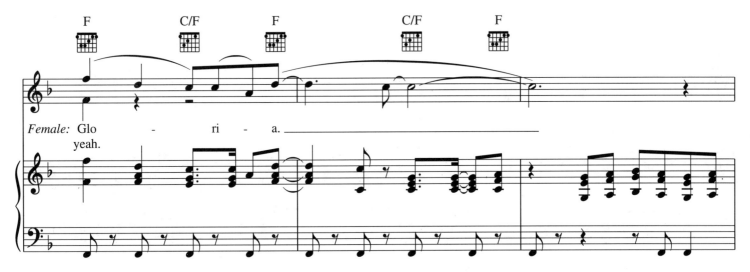

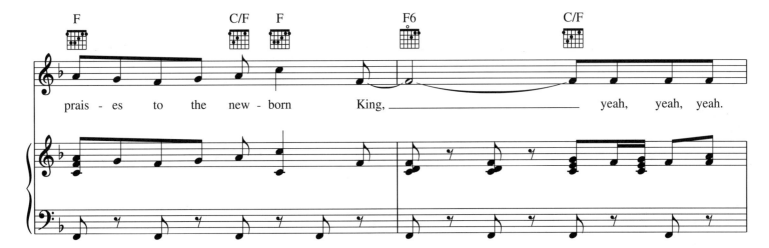

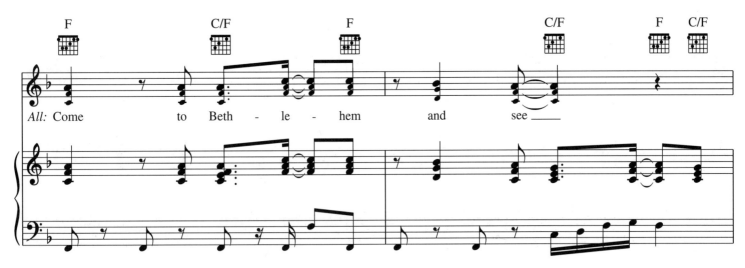

9

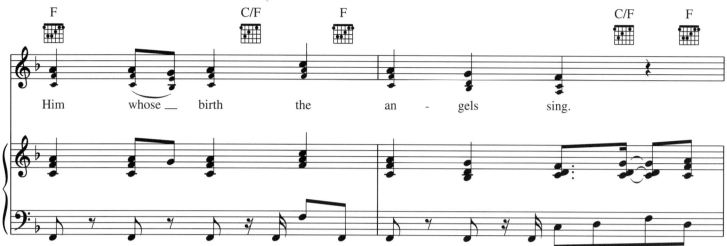

Him whose ___ birth the an - gels sing.

Come a - dore on ___ bend - ed knee

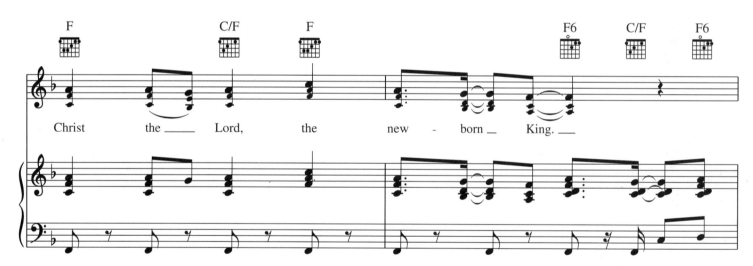

Christ the _____ Lord, the new - born ___ King. ___

Glo
(Glo - ri - a, glo - ri - a, ___ glo - ri - a,

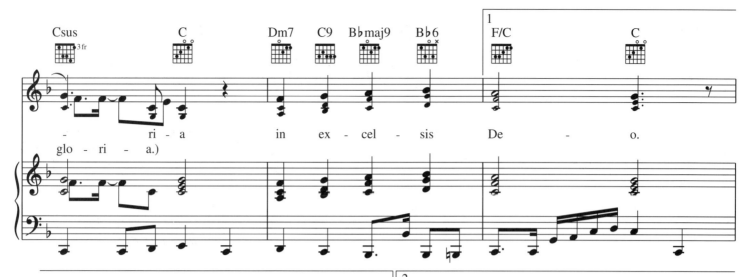

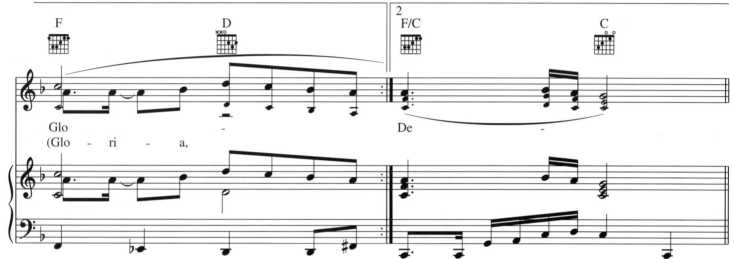

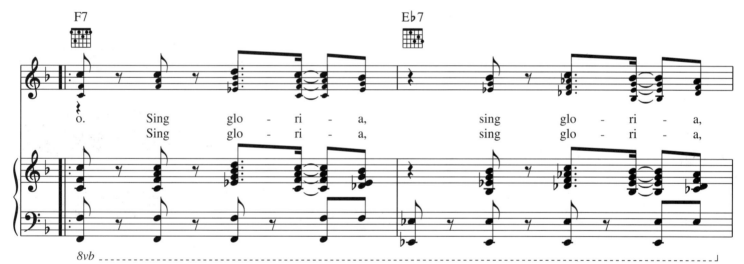

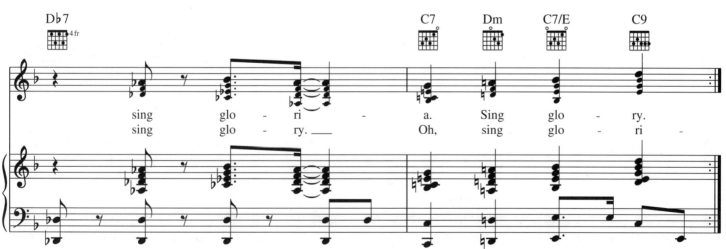

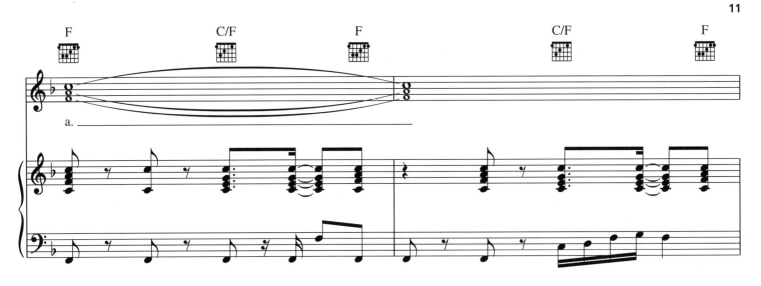

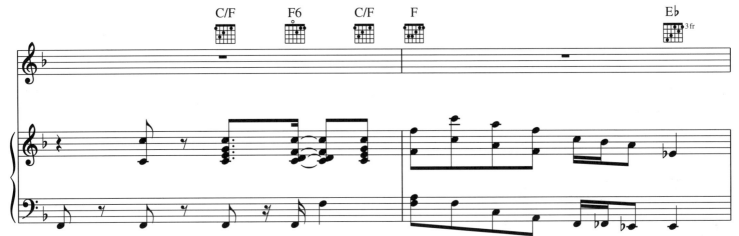

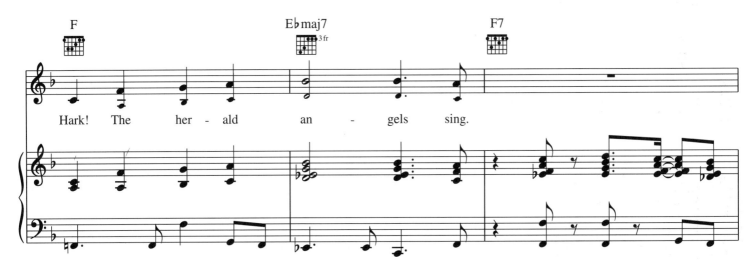

Hark! The her - ald an - gels sing.

Glo - ry to the new - born King. (New -

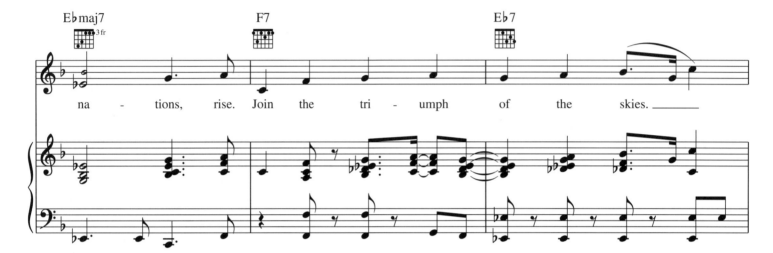

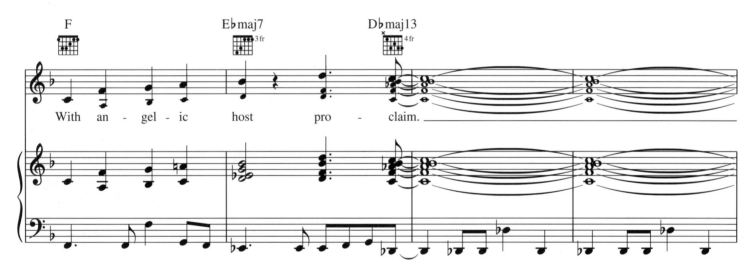

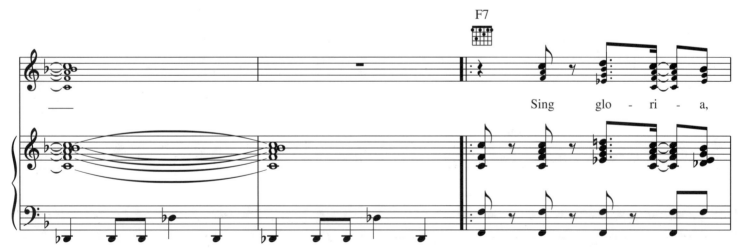

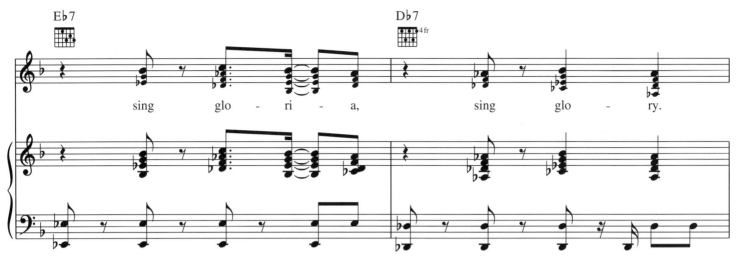

sing glo - ri - a, sing glo - ry.

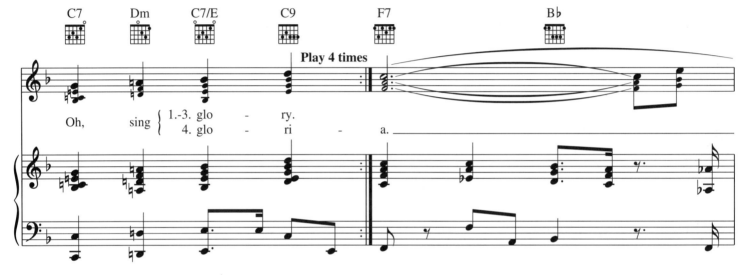

Oh, sing { 1.-3. glo - ry.
4. glo - ri - a. }

Play 4 times

1., 3. To the babe in a man - ger born _ a King.
2., 4. On the night in a sta - ble came _ a boy.

Glo - ri - a, hear the song the an - gels sing. Hear the moun - tains ech - o - ing.
Prince of Peace come to earth, the skies _ re - joice. Heav-en sings with a might-y voice, }

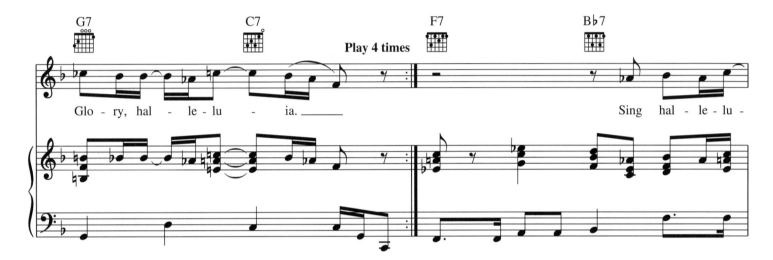

Play 4 times

Glo - ry, hal - le - lu - ia. _____ Sing hal - le - lu -

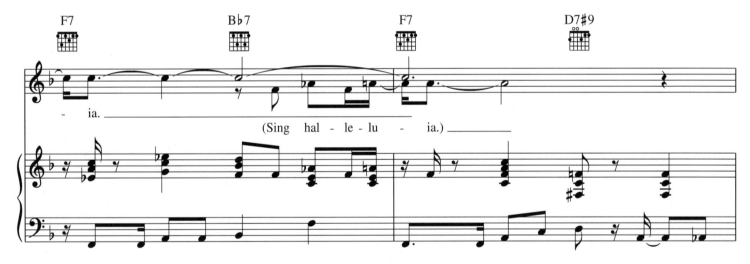

- ia. _____ (Sing hal - le - lu - ia.) _____

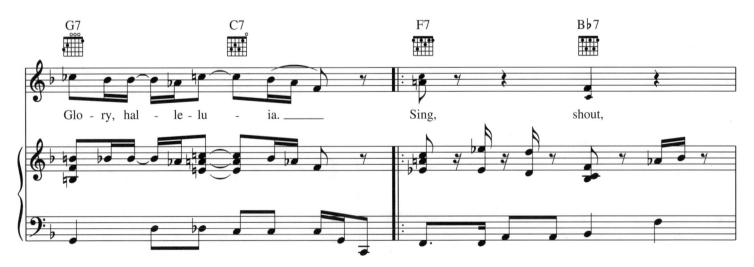

Glo - ry, hal - le - lu - ia. _____ Sing, shout,

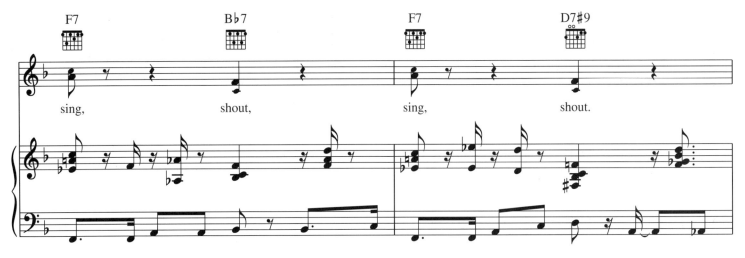

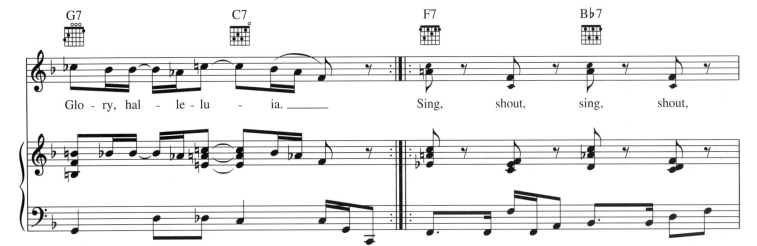

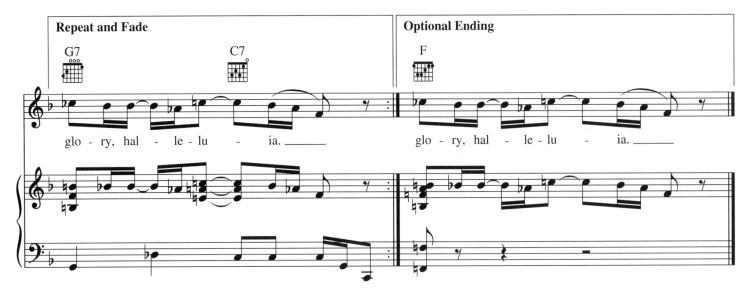

BABE IN THE STRAW

Words and Music by STEVE HINDALONG
and DERRI DAUGHERTY

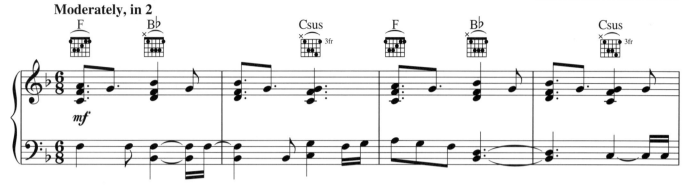

Who is this

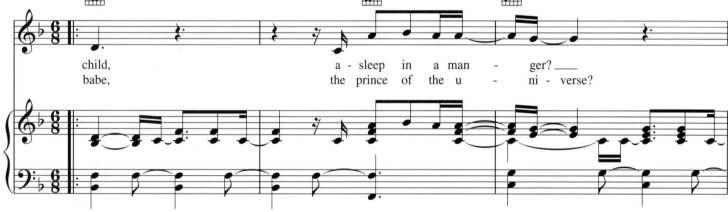

child,   a - sleep in a man - ger? ____
babe,   the prince of the u - ni - verse?

The heav - ens are bright, ____   and the sta - ble's so ____
The don - key is bray - ing,   the an - gels are

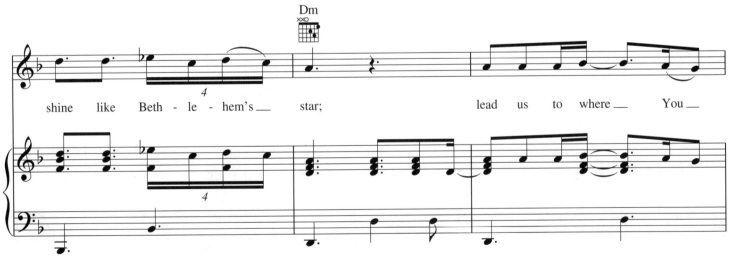

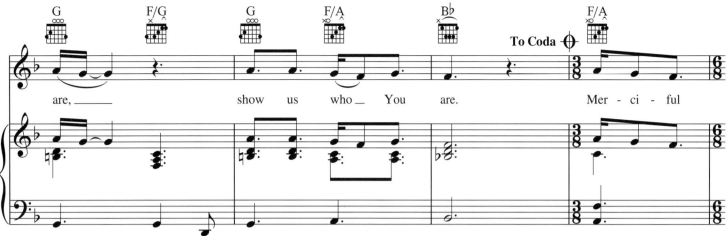

are, _____ show us who _ You are. Mer - ci - ful

one, lov - er of ev - 'ry soul,

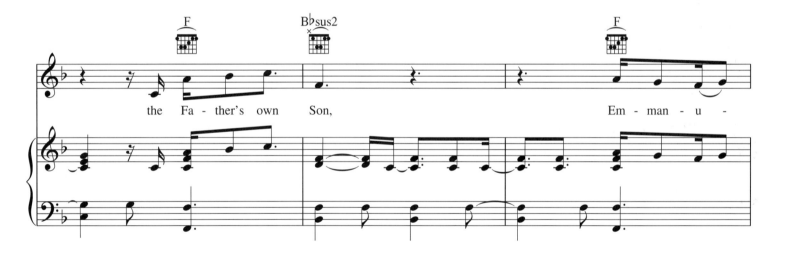

the Fa - ther's own Son, Em - man - u -

el. Yes, we be - lieve _____

You are a - ble to heal _____ us.   No - el, no -

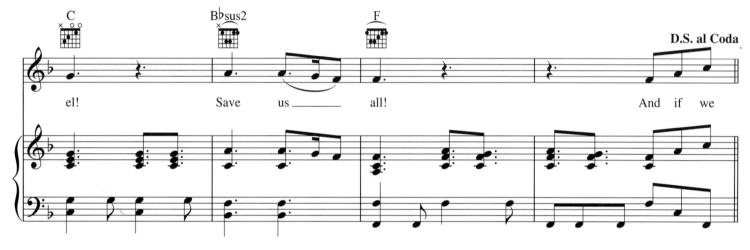

el!   Save   us _____ all!   And if we

CODA

Save us to - night, _____   lit - tle

babe in the straw. __   Save us to - night. __

BREATH OF HEAVEN
(Mary's Song)

Words and Music by AMY GRANT
and CHRIS EATON

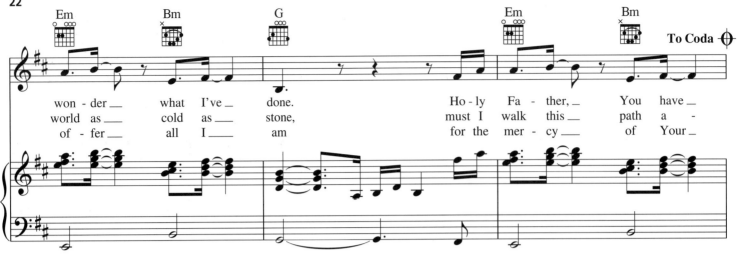

won - der ___ what I've ___ done.   Ho - ly Fa - ther, ___ You have ___
world as ___ cold as ___ stone,   must I walk this ___ path a -
of - fer ___ all I ___ am   for the mer - cy ___ of Your ___

come ___ and cho - sen me now ___ to car - ry Your

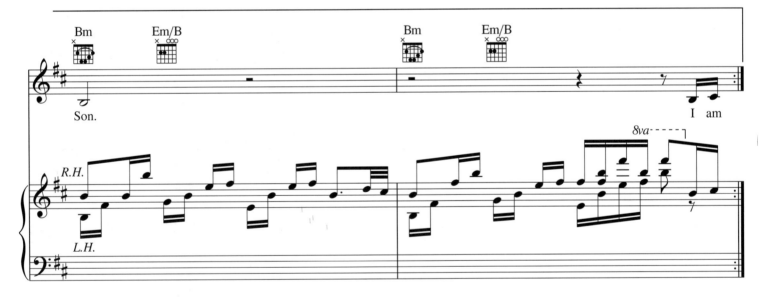

Son. ___   I am

lone. ___   Be ___ with me now, ___   be ___ with me

CODA

plan. _____ Help _____ me be strong, _____ help _____ me be... _____

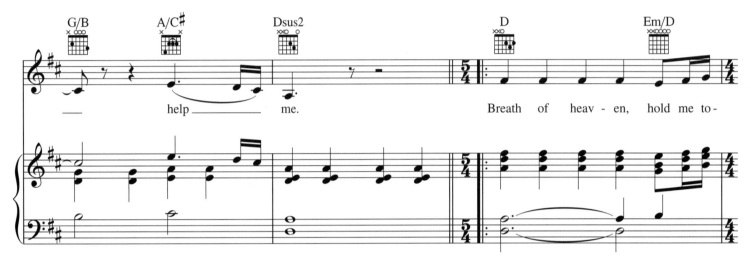

_____ help _____ me. Breath of heav - en, hold me to-

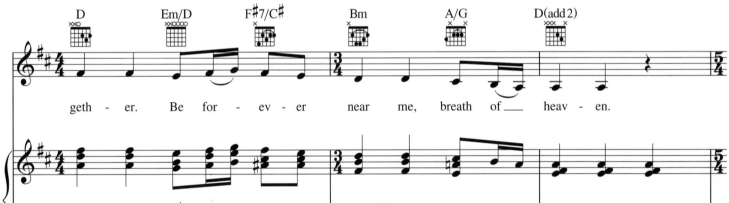

geth - er. Be for - ev - er near me, breath of ___ heav - en.

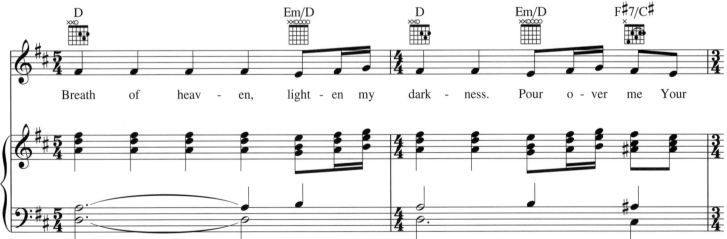

Breath of heav - en, light - en my dark - ness. Pour o - ver me Your

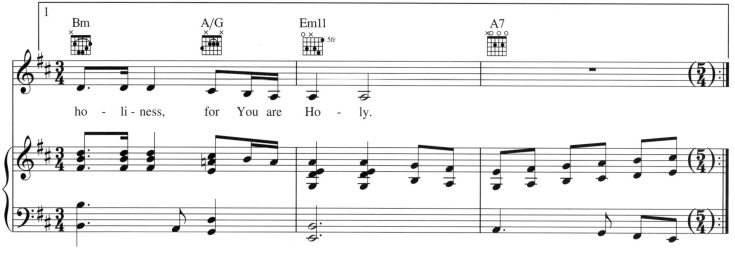

ho - li - ness, for You are Ho - ly.

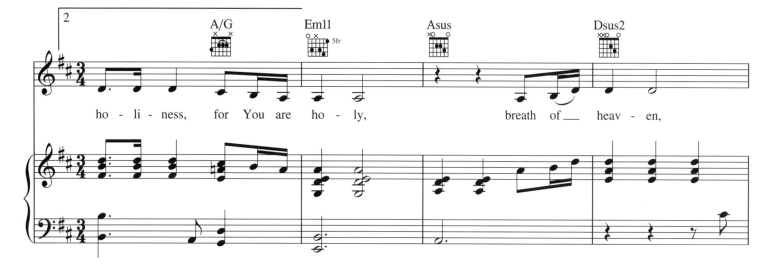

ho - li - ness, for You are ho - ly, breath of ___ heav - en,

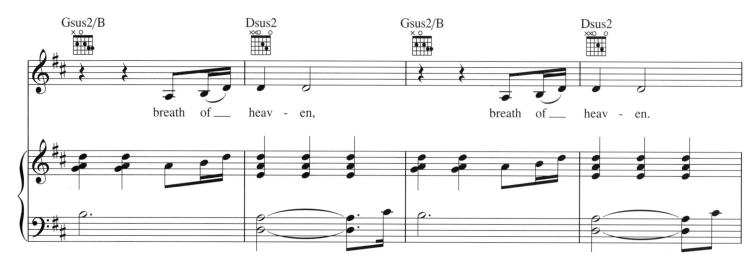

breath of ___ heav - en, breath of ___ heav - en.

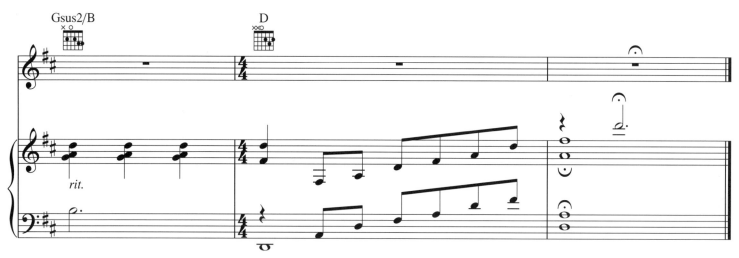

rit.

CALL HIS NAME JESUS

Words and Music by
SHAWN CRAIG

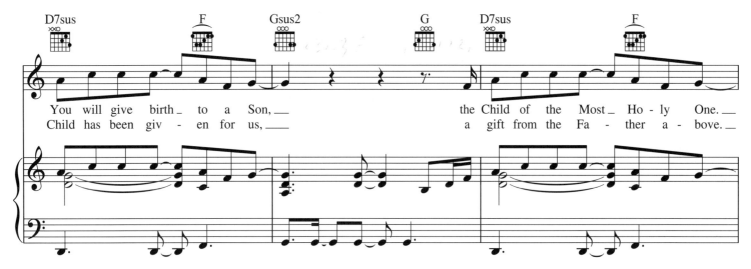

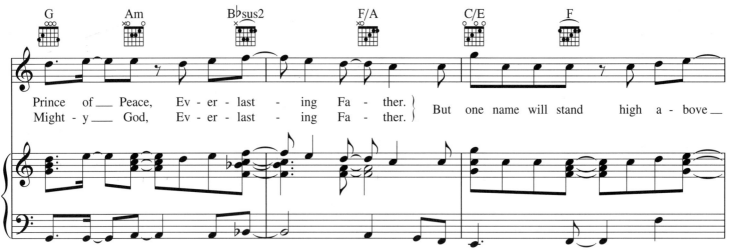

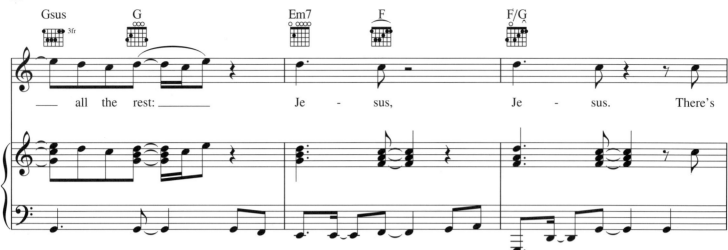

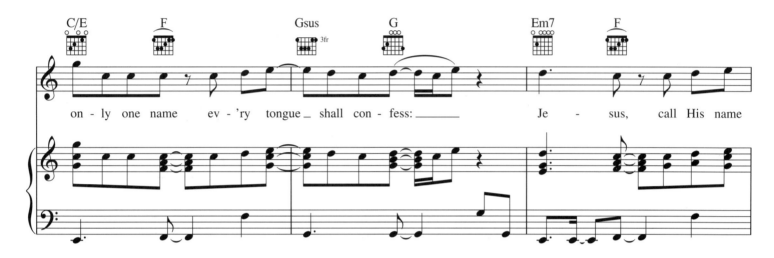

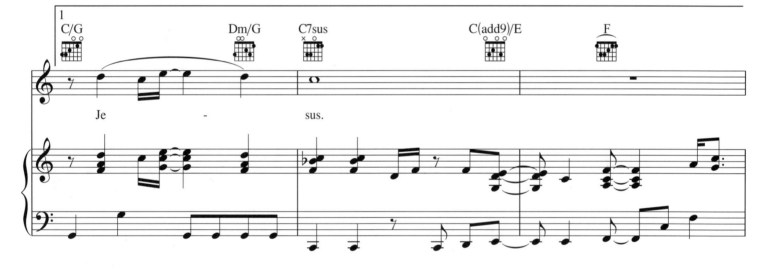

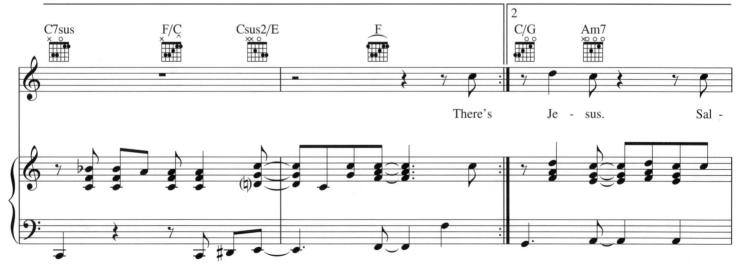

va - tion, heal - ing and grace _____ in the name a - bove _ all _ names. _

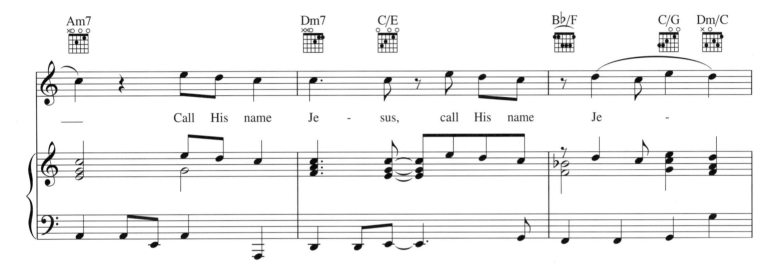

_ Call His name Je - sus, call His name Je -

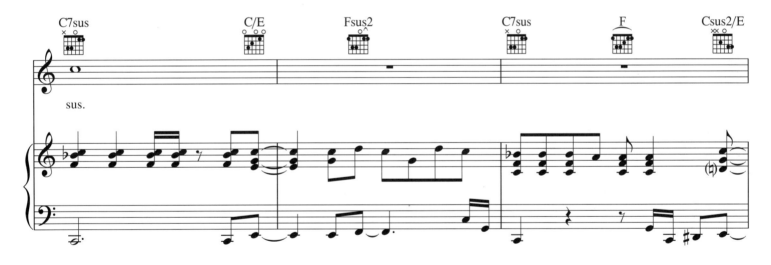

sus.

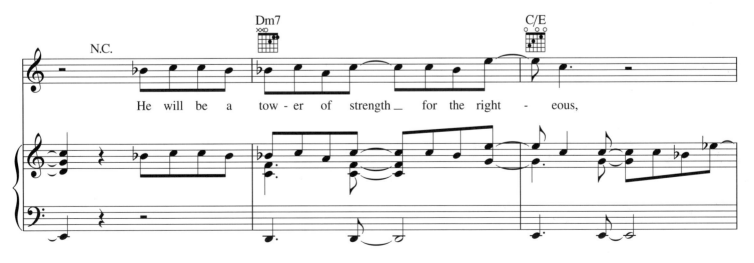

He will be a tow - er of strength _ for the right - eous,

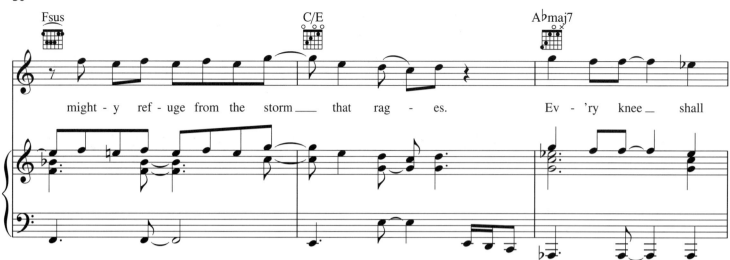

might-y ref-uge from the storm ___ that rag-es. Ev-'ry knee ___ shall

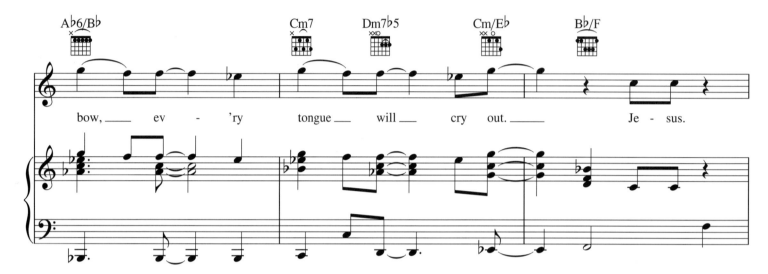

bow, ___ ev-'ry tongue ___ will ___ cry out. ___ Je-sus.

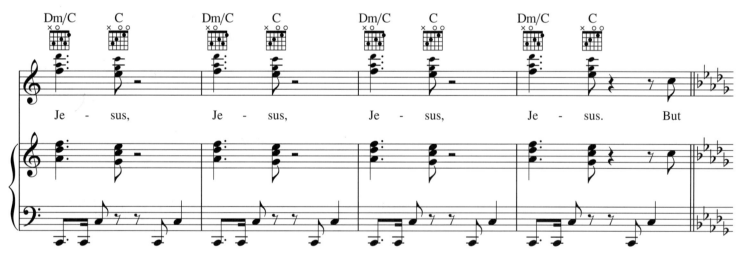

Je-sus, Je-sus, Je-sus, Je-sus. But

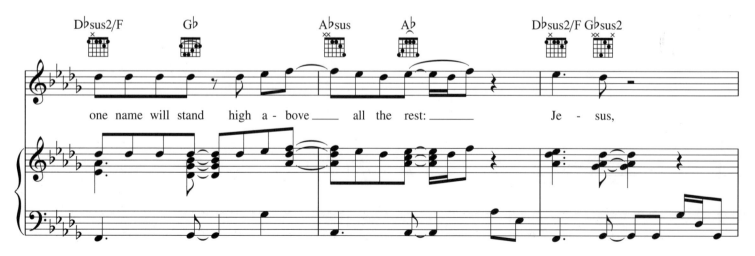

one name will stand high a-bove ___ all the rest: _____ Je-sus,

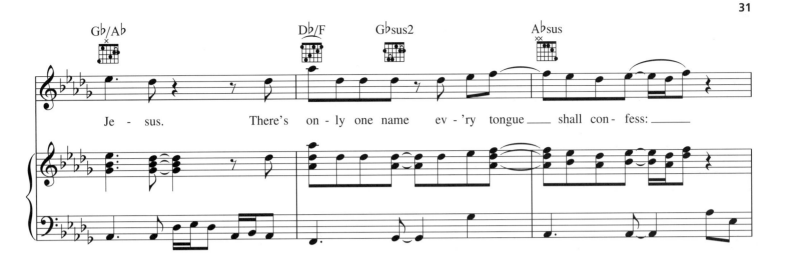

Je - sus. There's on - ly one name ev - 'ry tongue shall con - fess:

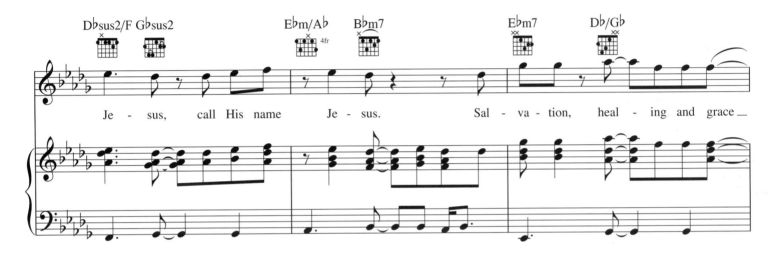

Je - sus, call His name Je - sus. Sal - va - tion, heal - ing and grace

in the name a - bove all names. Call His name

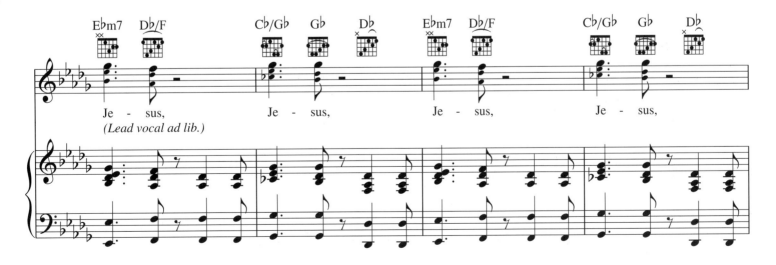

Je - sus, Je - sus, Je - sus, Je - sus,
(Lead vocal ad lib.)

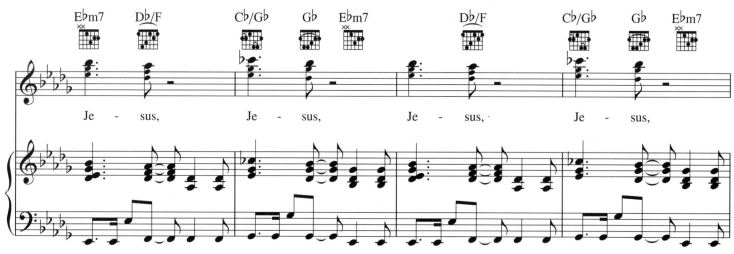

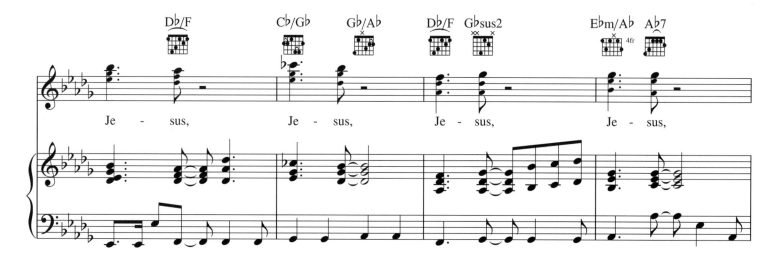

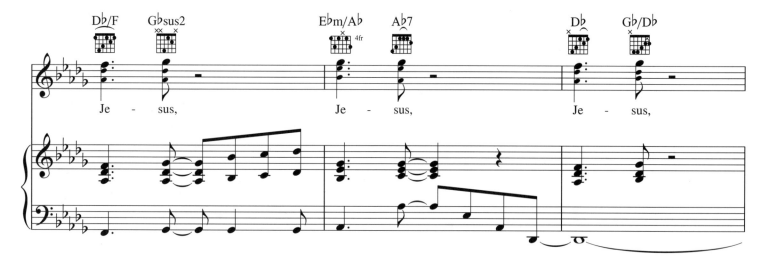

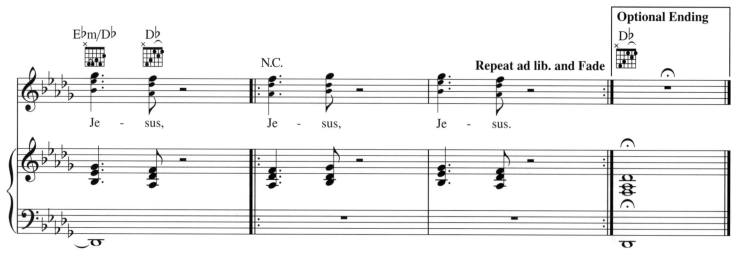

CHILD OF LOVE

Words and Music by STEVE HINDALONG,
MARK D. LEE and MATTHEW WEST

Moderately slow, in 2

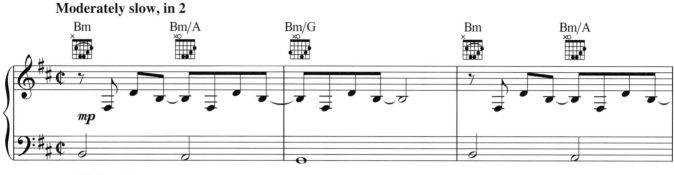

With pedal

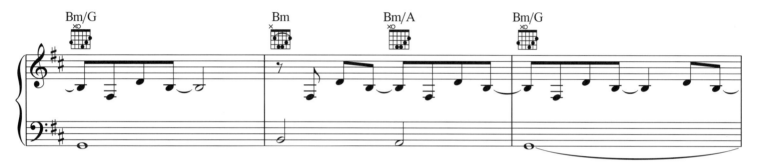

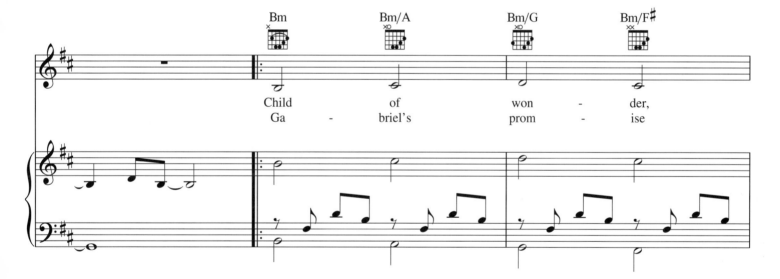

Child of won - der,
Ga - briel's prom - ise

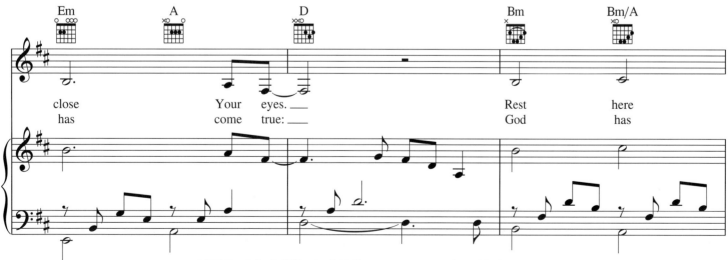

close Your eyes. ___ Rest here
has come true: ___ God has

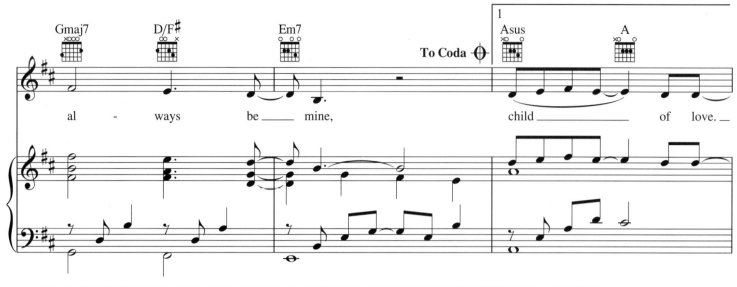

al - ways be ___ mine, child _____ of love. ___

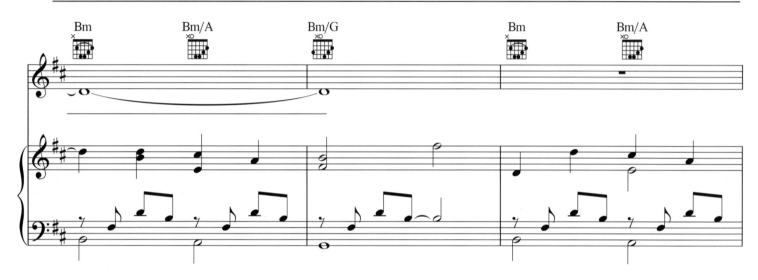

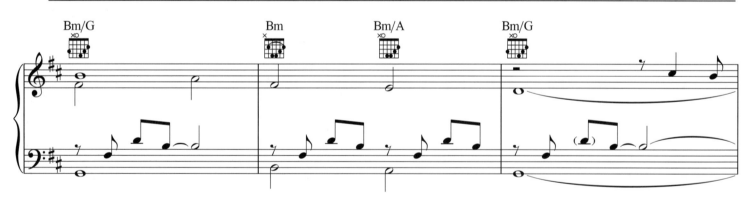

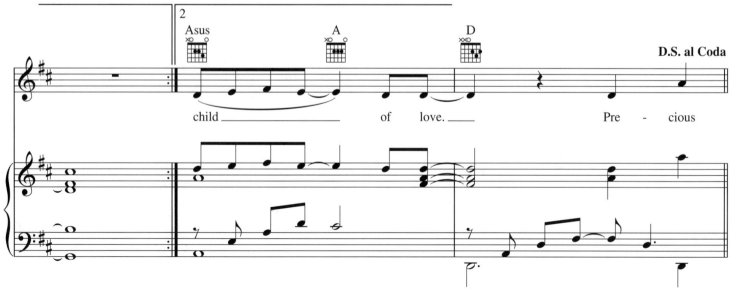

child _____ of love. ___ Pre - cious

CHRISTMAS IS ALL IN THE HEART

Words and Music by
STEVEN CURTIS CHAPMAN

- lie Brown's. __ And un-der-neath there's one lit-tle gift __ for
__ of dawn __ with Mom and Dad and cam - 'ras mak - in'

him, and one lit-tle gift __ for her. __
sure we'd nev - er for - get __ that day. __

Af-ter six months on __ the new __
Now I'm the one who's tak - in' pic -

__ job, they're still bare - ly get - tin' by. So, in the way of dec - o - ra -
- tures in the mid - dle of __ the night of my own __ blonde-head - ed

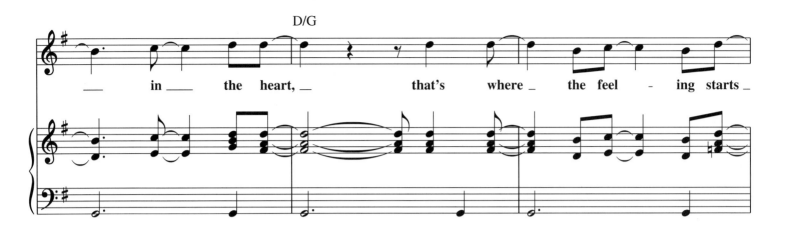

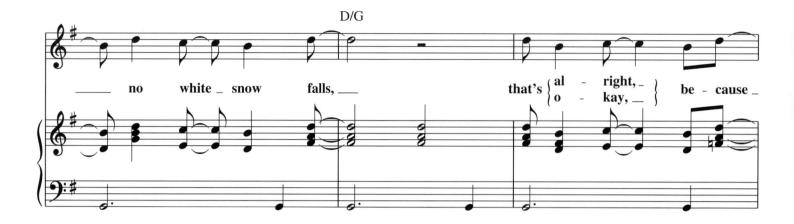

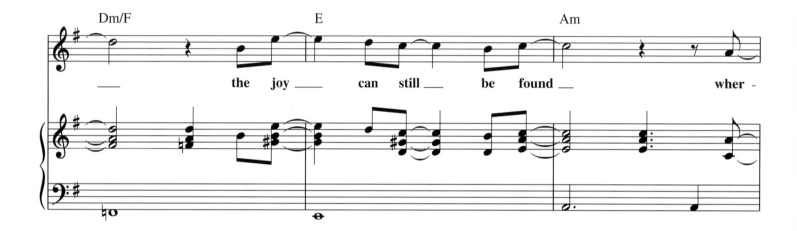

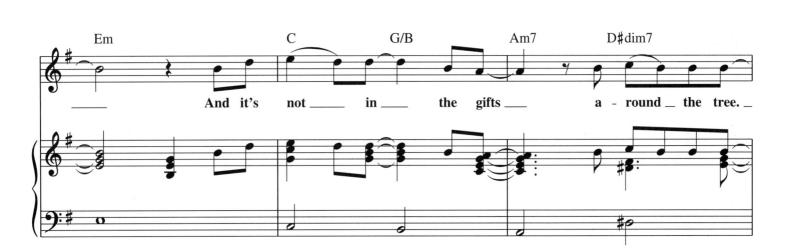

night our Sav - ior came. __ And that __ same Love __ can still be found __

__ wher - ev - er you are _____ 'cause

Christ - mas __ is all _____ in ___ the heart. __ And the joy __

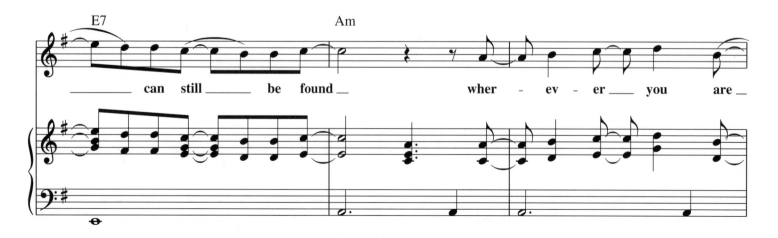

_____ can still _____ be found __ wher - ev - er ___ you are __

'cause Christ - mas __ is all, _____

all in ___ the ___ heart. __

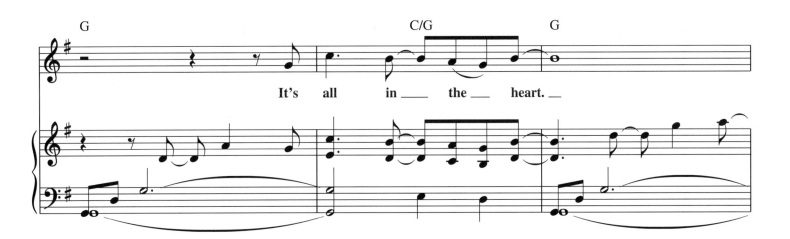

It's all in ___ the ___ heart. __

rit.

COME EMMANUEL

Words and Music by
TWILA PARIS

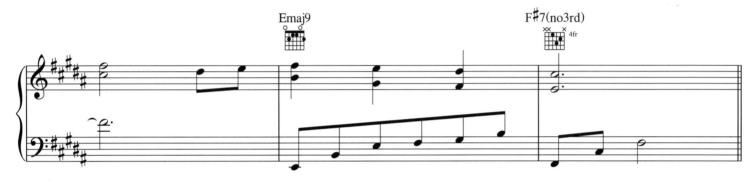

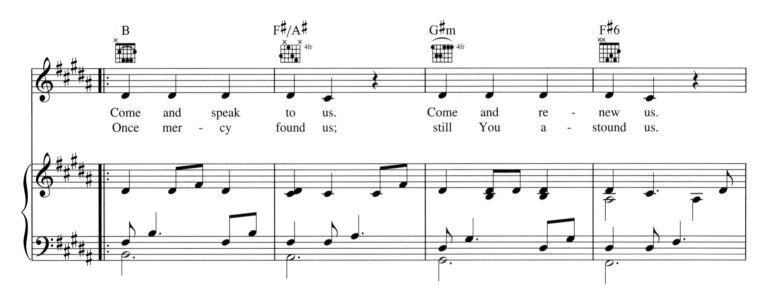

Come and speak to us. Come and re - new us.
Once mer - cy found us; still You a - stound us.

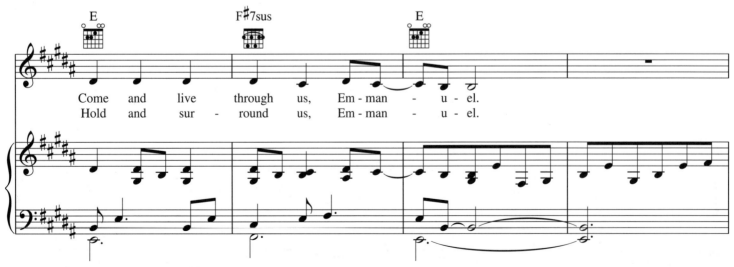

Come and live through us, Em - man - u - el.
Hold and sur - round us, Em - man - u - el.

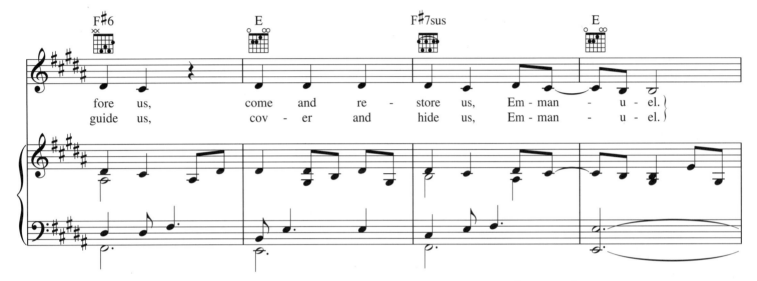

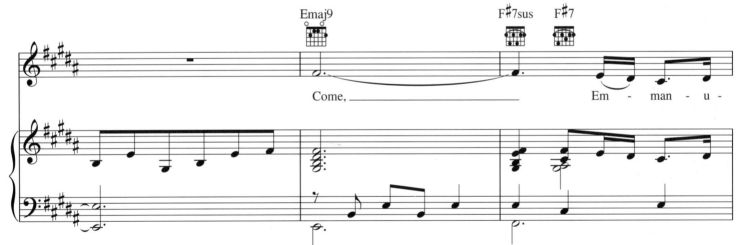

Come and speak to us, fill and re -

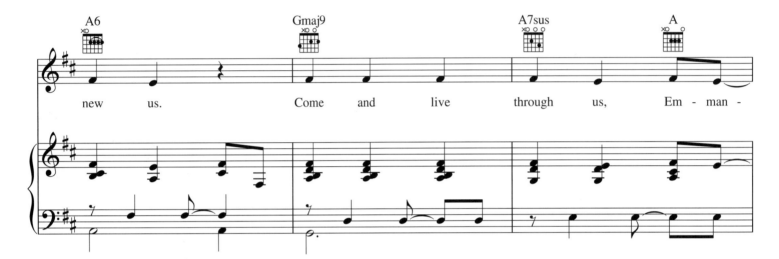

new us. Come and live through us, Em - man -

- u - el, _____ Em - man - u - el, _____ Em - man -

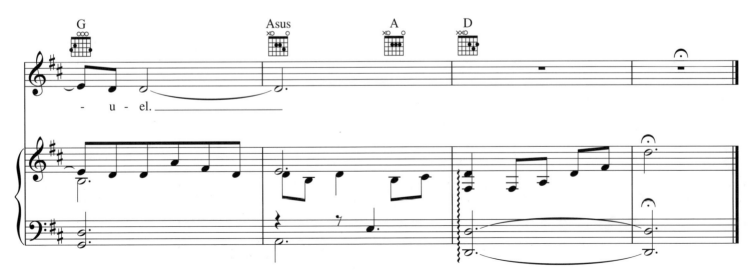

- u - el. _____

A CRADLE PRAYER

Words and Music by REBECCA ST. JAMES
and CHARLES GARRETT

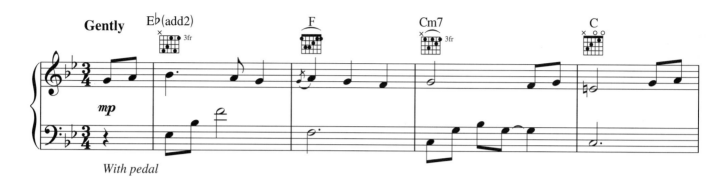

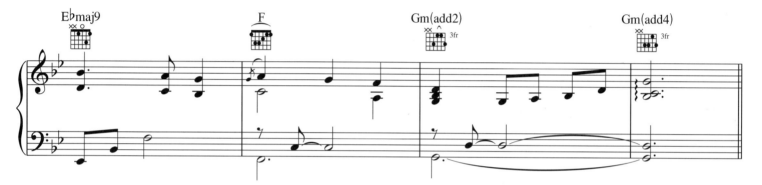

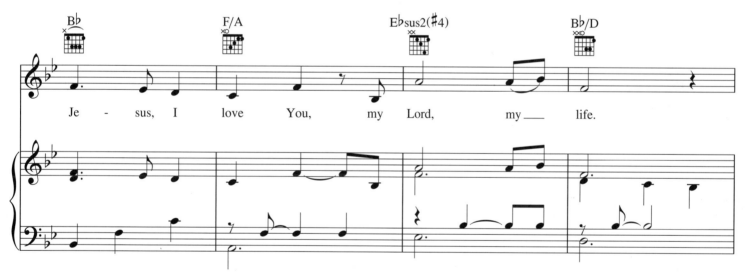

Je - sus, I love You, my Lord, my ___ life.

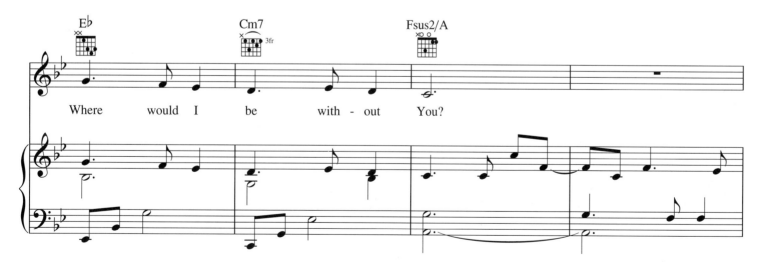

Where would I be with - out You?

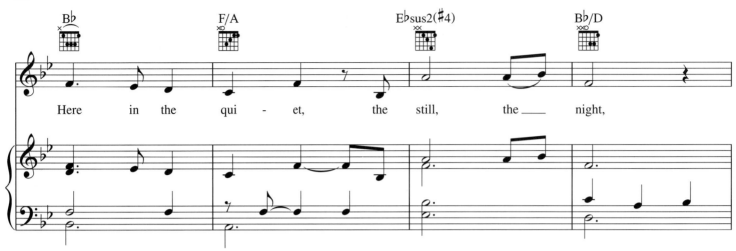

Here in the qui - et, the still, the ___ night,

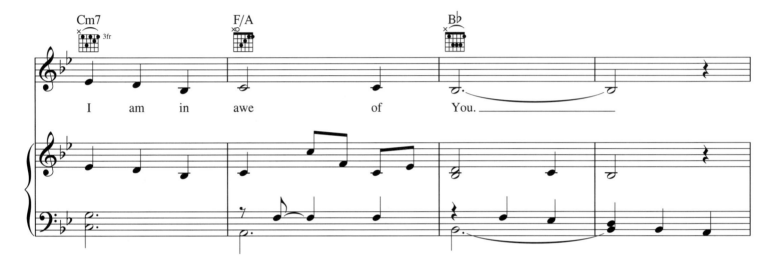

I am in awe of You. ___

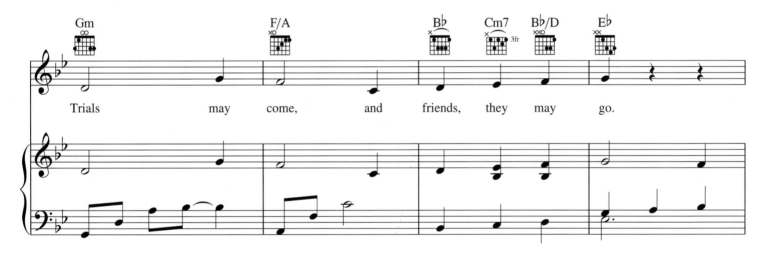

Trials may come, and friends, they may go.

What real - ly mat - ters is You, my ___ Lord.

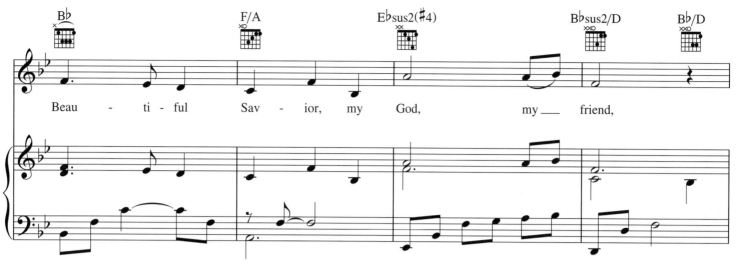

Beau - ti - ful Sav - ior, my God, my __ friend,

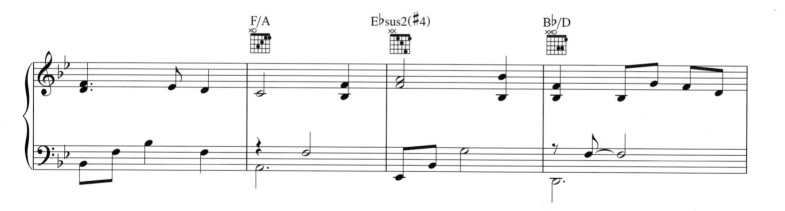

I am in awe of You. _____

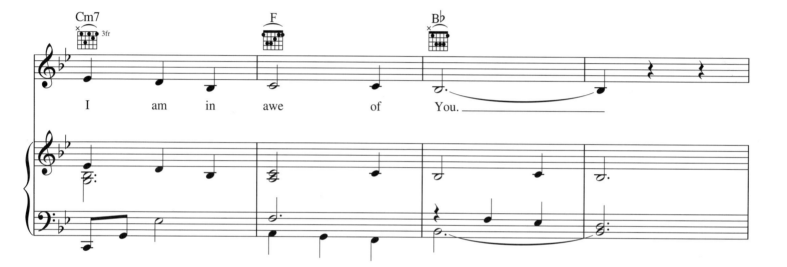

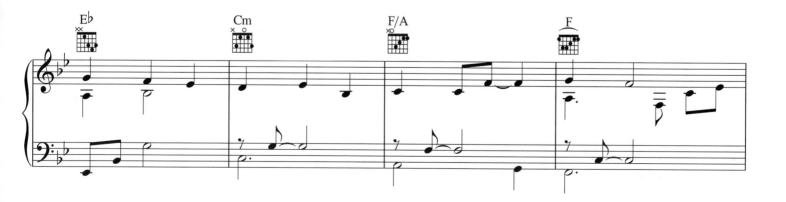

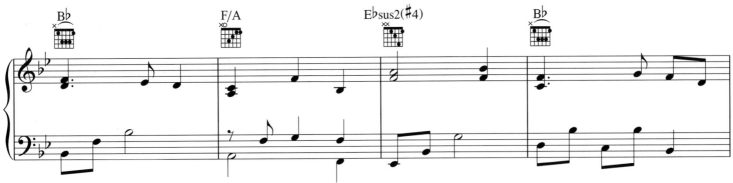

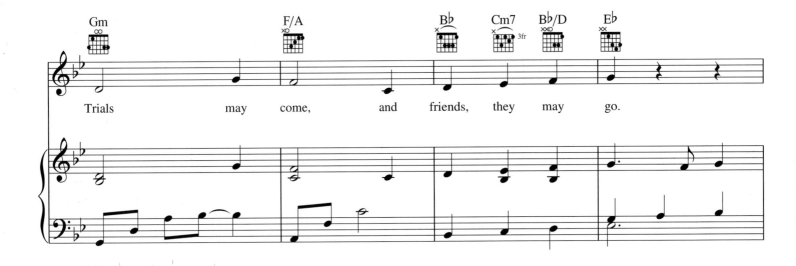

Trials may come, and friends, they may go.

What real - ly mat - ters is You, my ___ Lord. ___

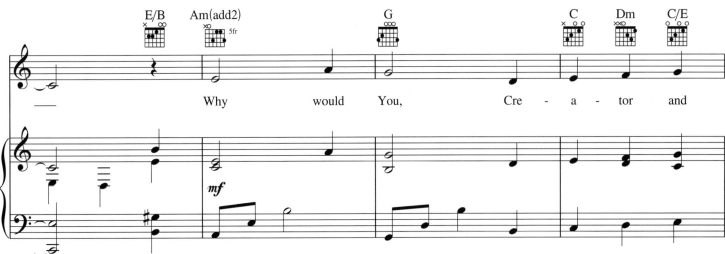

Why would You, Cre - a - tor and

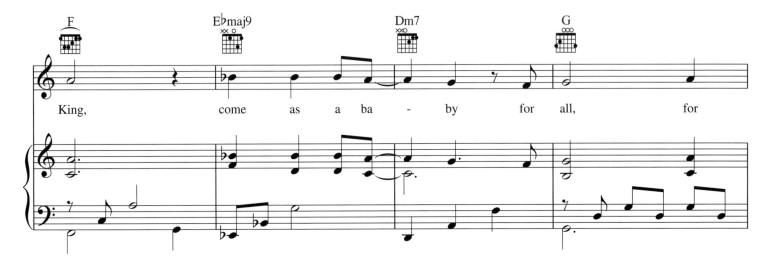

King, come as a ba - by for all, for

me? _____ Beau - ti - ful

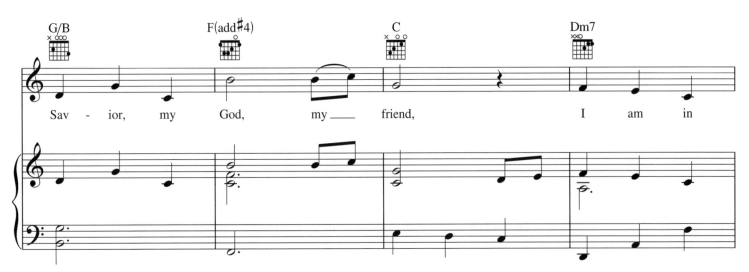

Sav - ior, my God, my ___ friend, I am in

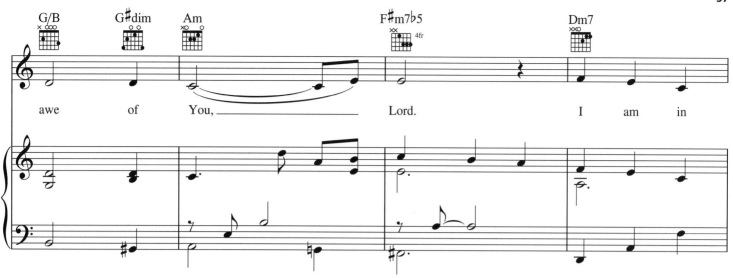

awe   of   You, _____ Lord.   I   am   in

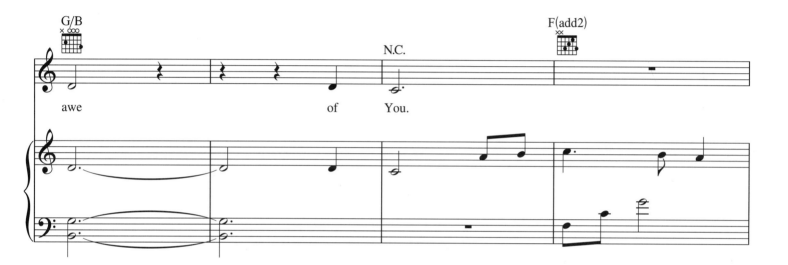

awe   of   You.

EMMANUEL

Words and Music by
MICHAEL W. SMITH

Steadily

N.C.

Em - man - u - el, Em -

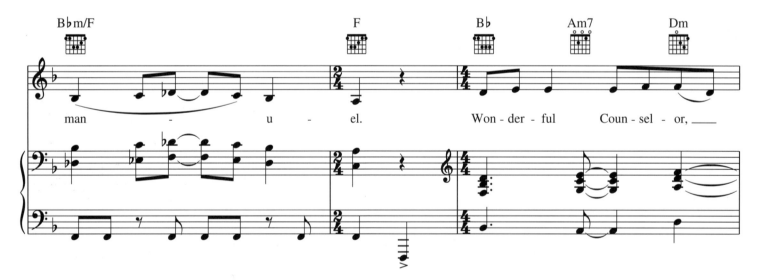

man - u - el. Won - der - ful Coun - sel - or, _____

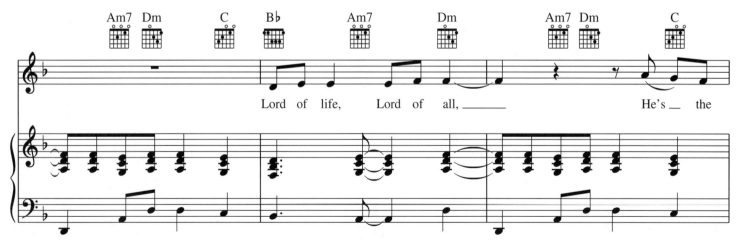

Lord of life, Lord of all, _____ He's _ the

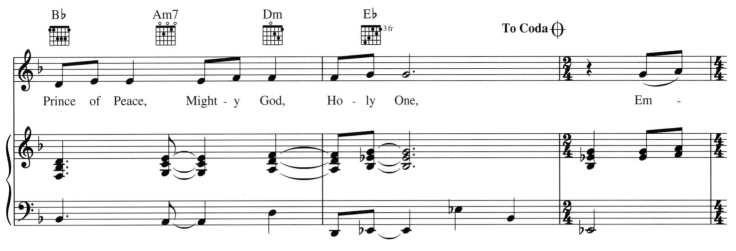

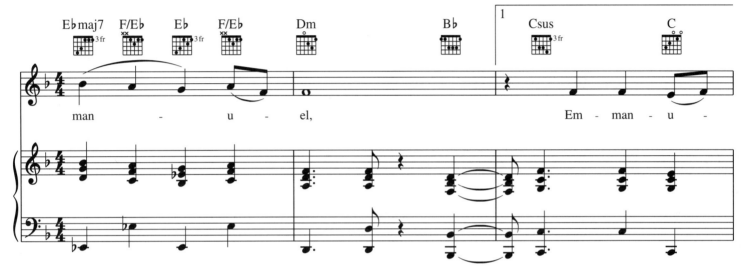

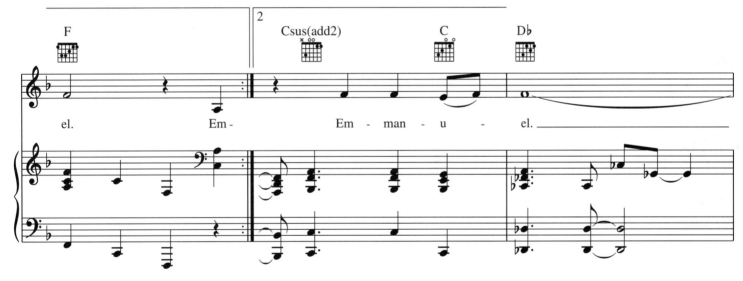

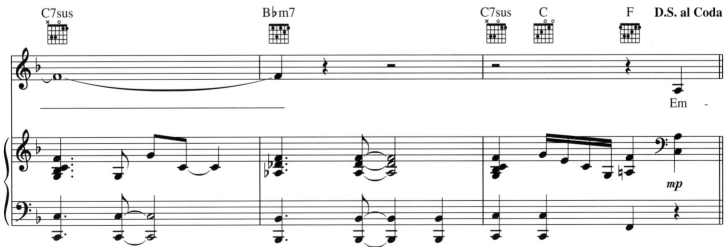

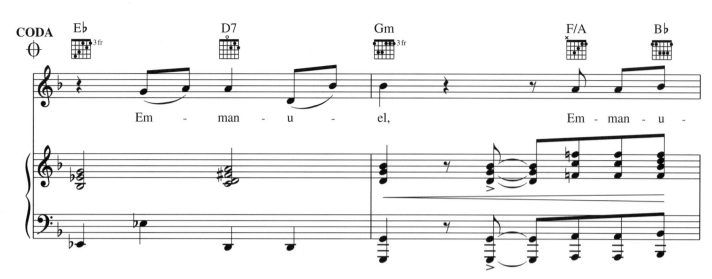

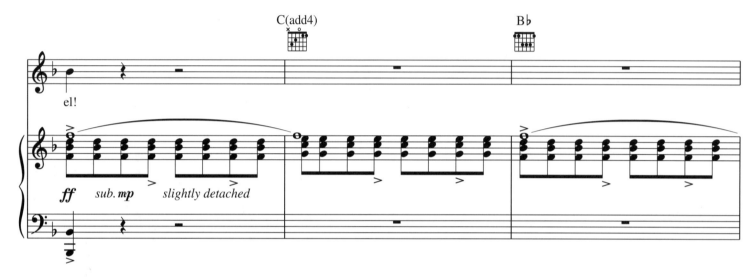

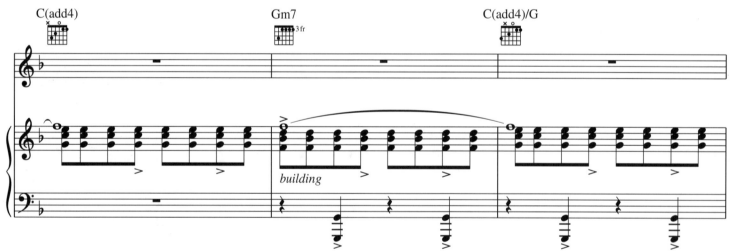

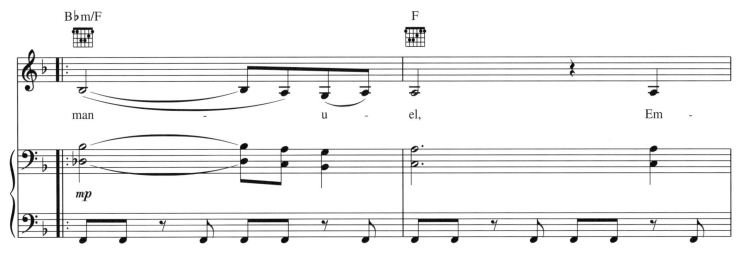

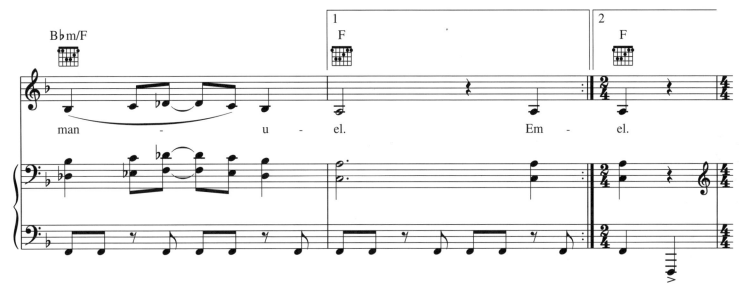

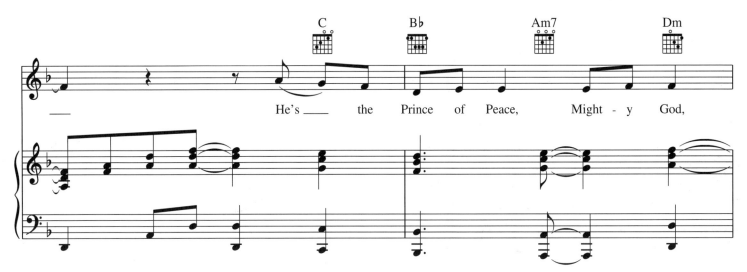

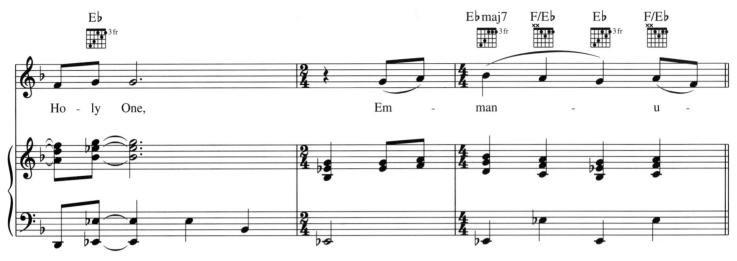

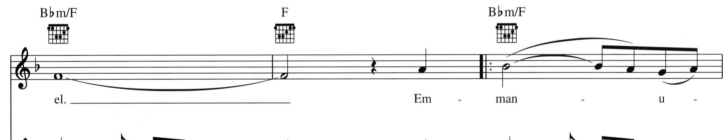

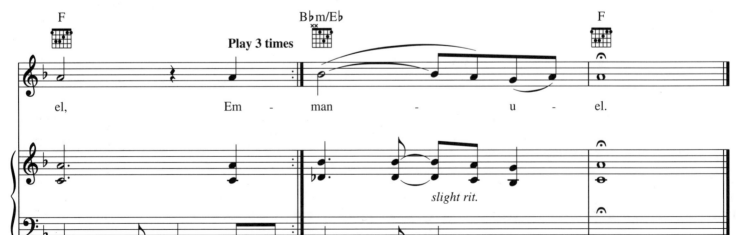

GLORIA

Words and Music by MICHAEL W. SMITH
Based on "Angels We Have Heard On High"

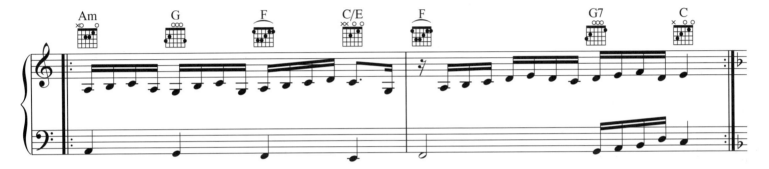

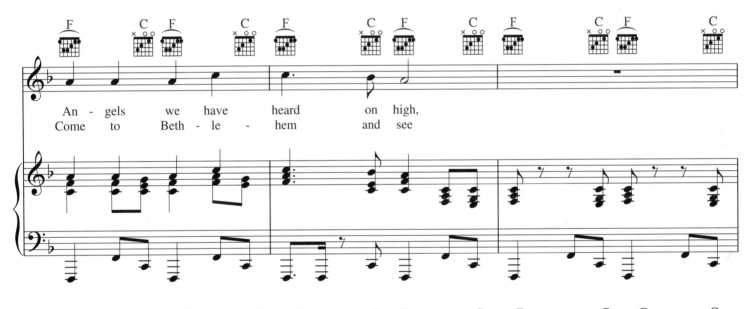

An - gels we have heard on high,
Come to we Beth - le - hem and see

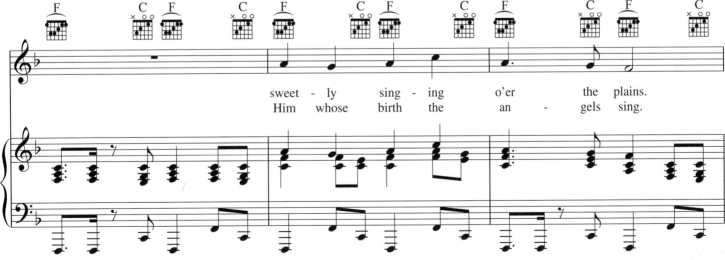

sweet - ly sing - ing o'er the plains.
Him whose birth the an - gels sing.

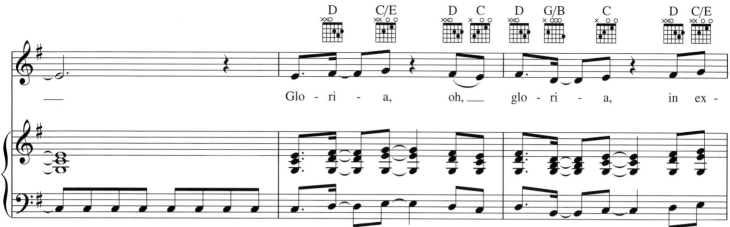

Glo - ri - a, oh, __ glo - ri - a, in ex -

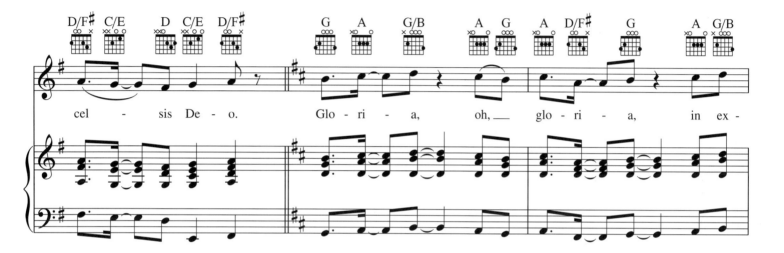

cel - sis De - o. Glo - ri - a, oh, __ glo - ri - a, in ex -

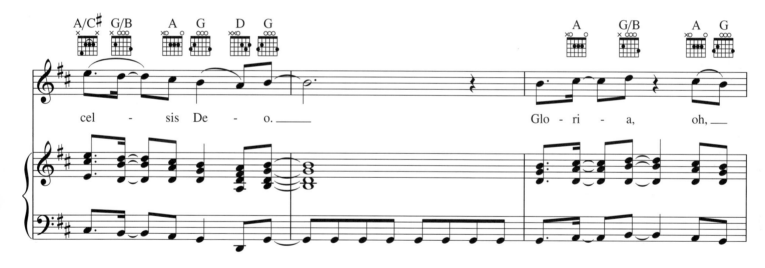

cel - sis De - o. ___ Glo - ri - a, oh, __

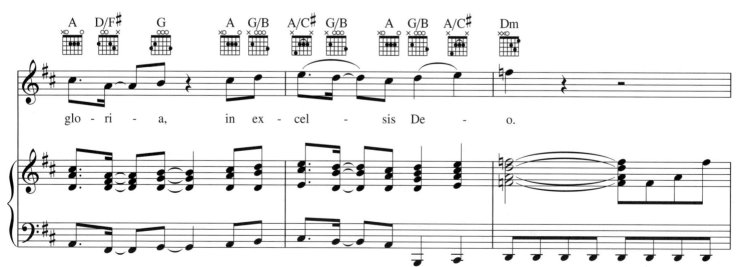

glo - ri - a, in ex - cel - sis De - o.

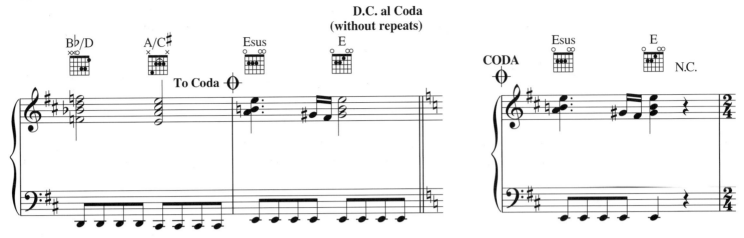

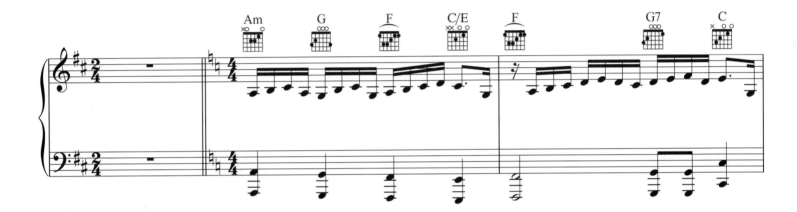

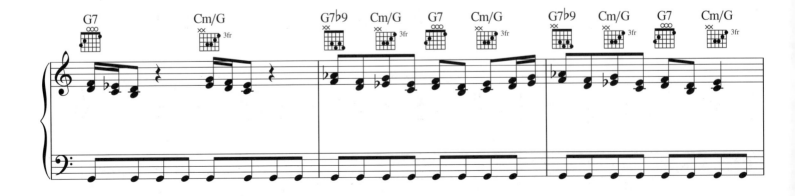

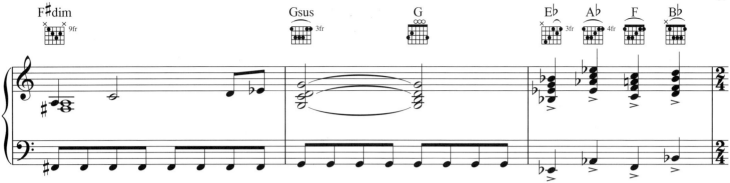

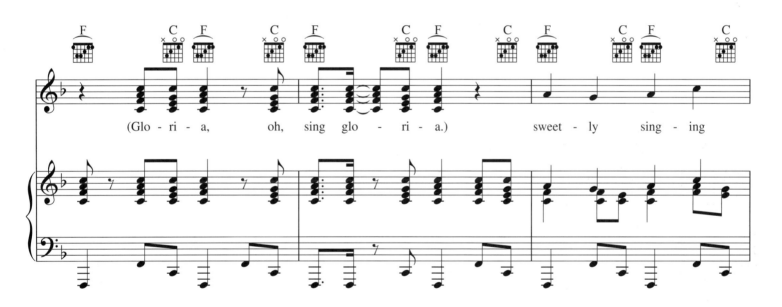

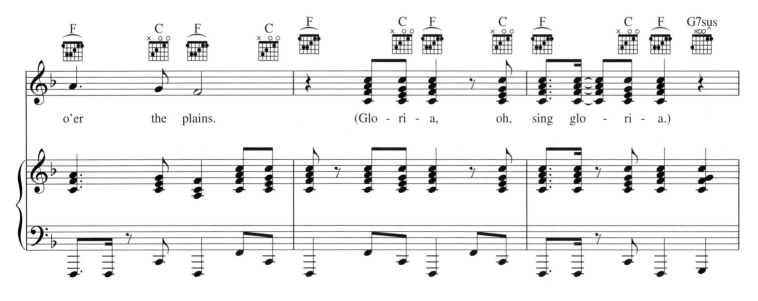

Je - sus, Lord of heav'n and earth;

with us sing our Sav - ior's birth.

Glo - ri - a, oh, ___ glo - ri - a, in ex - cel - sis De - o.

__ Glo - ri - a, oh, ___ glo - ri - a, in ex -

cel - sis De - o. _____ Glo - ri - a, oh, _____

glo - ri - a, in ex - cel - sis De - o. Glo - ri - a, oh, _____

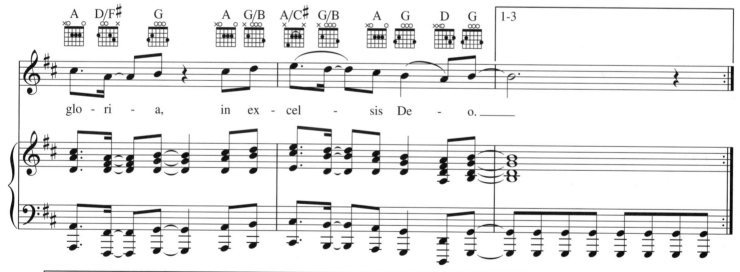

glo - ri - a, in ex - cel - sis De - o. _____

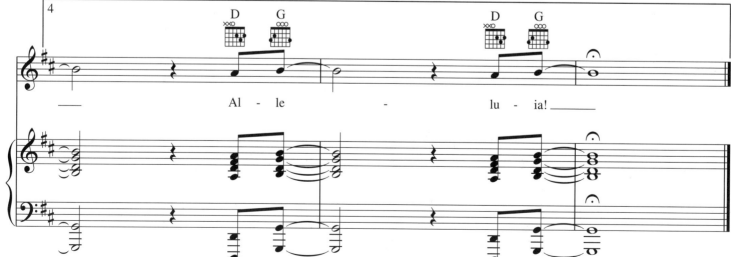

_____ Al - le - lu - ia! _____

EMMANUEL HAS COME

Words and Music by
DON MOEN

Christ-mas is a-bout His glo-ry, Christ-mas is a-bout His grace.
An-gels fill the night with sing-ing; God is reach-ing out to man,

Christ-mas is a gift of love our Fa-ther gave us.
bring-ing us a gift of hope in Christ, our Sav-ior.

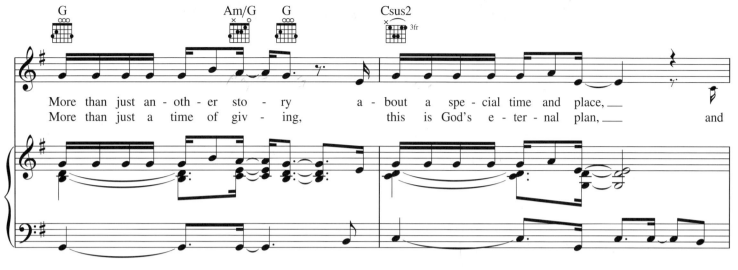

More than just an-oth-er sto-ry a-bout a spe-cial time and place, ___
More than just a time of giv-ing, this is God's e-ter-nal plan, ___ and

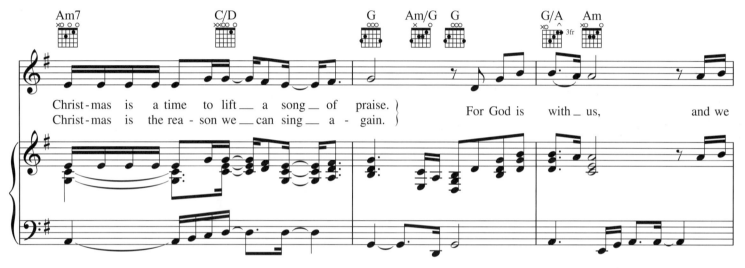

Christ-mas is a time to lift ___ a song ___ of praise. } For God is with ___ us, and we
Christ-mas is the rea-son we ___ can sing ___ a-gain. }

cel-e-brate ___ the glo-ry of His pres-ence. Christ has come ___

___ to fill our hearts ___ with love. He came to save ___ us; King of

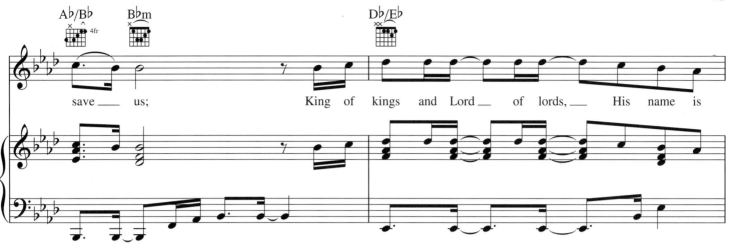

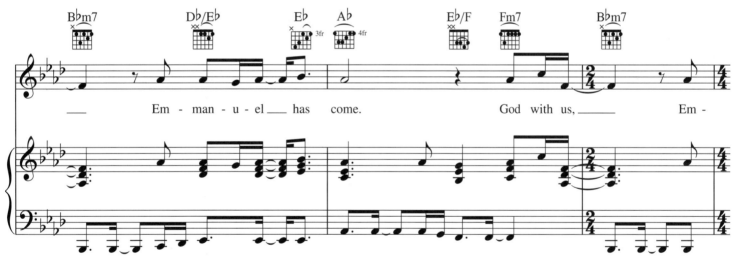

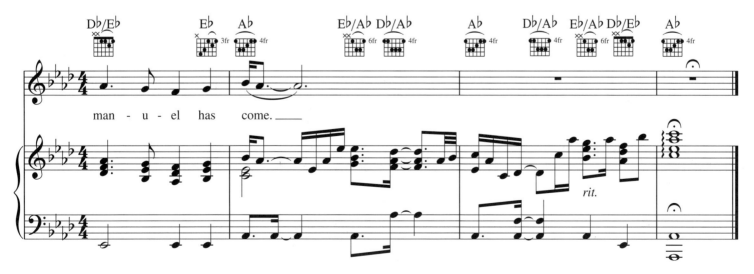

GOOD NEWS

Words and Music by
ROB MATHES

Moderately, with expression

Original key: A♭ major. This edition has been transposed down one half-step to be more playable.

81

JOY
(To the World)

Words and Music by DAN MUCKALA,
GRANT CUNNINGHAM and BROWN BANNISTER

D.S. al Coda

HALLELUJAH

Words and Music by
DARLENE ZSCHECH

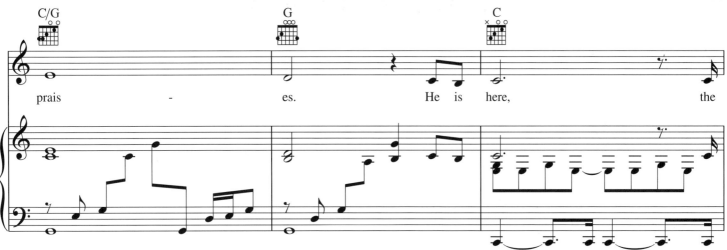

prais - es. He is here, the

prom - ise of ___ the King. ___ To You our lives ___ we

bring. Let Your glo - ry be ___ re - vealed. ___

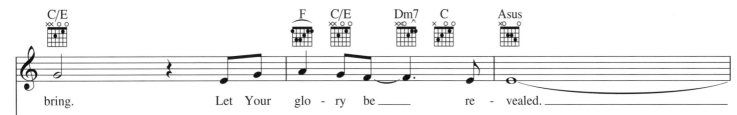

___ Joy to the world! ___

cresc.   mf

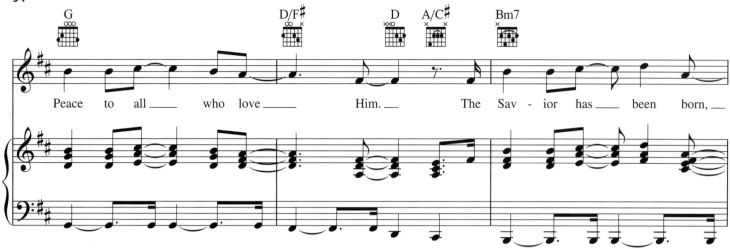

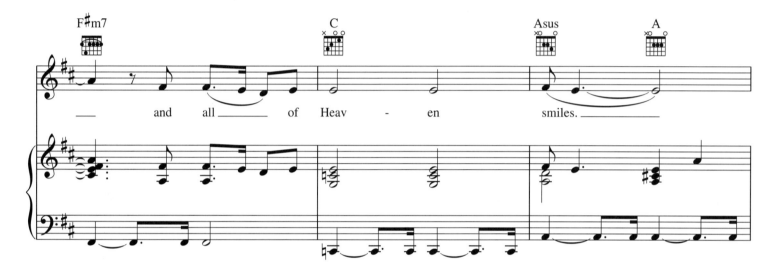

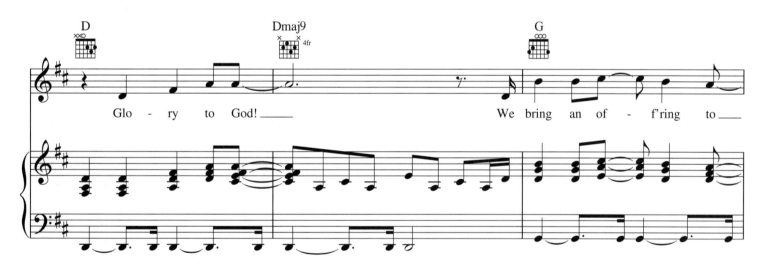

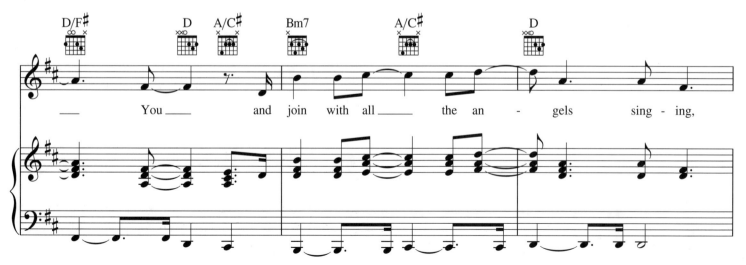

HOLY CHILD

Words and Music by ROB MATHES
and PHIL NAISH

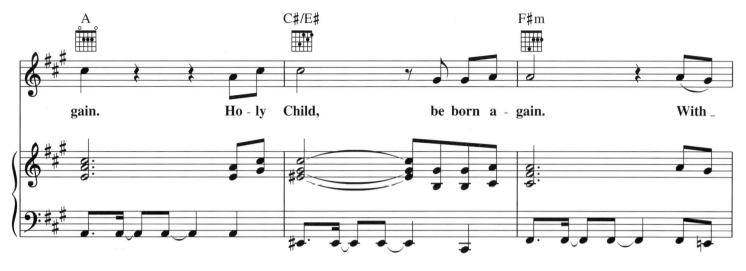

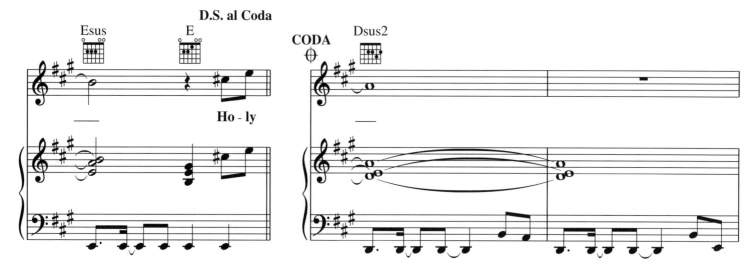

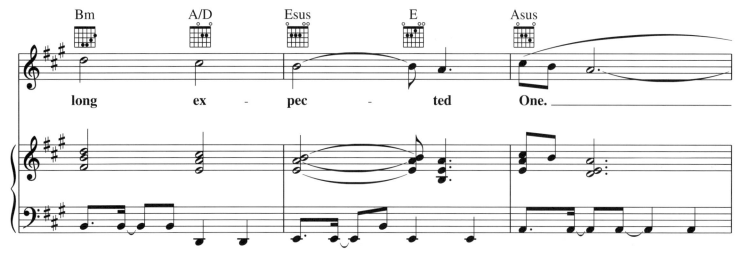

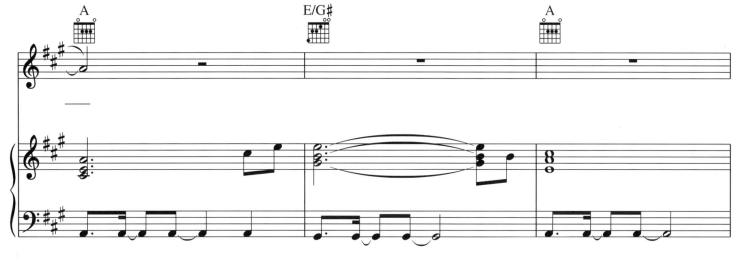

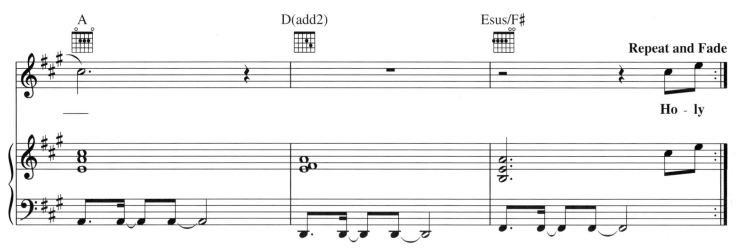

A KING IS BORN

Words and Music by SY GORIEB
and TIM HOSMAN

A King __ is born, ah - ooh, hal - le - lu - jah!

a cappella

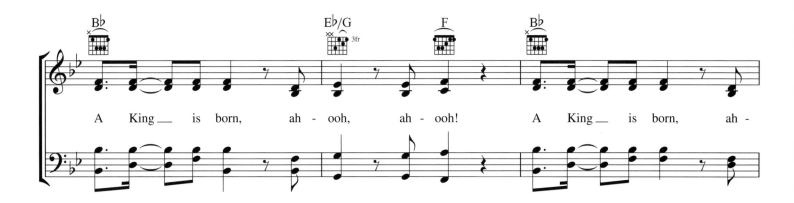

A King __ is born, ah - ooh, ah - ooh! A King __ is born, ah -

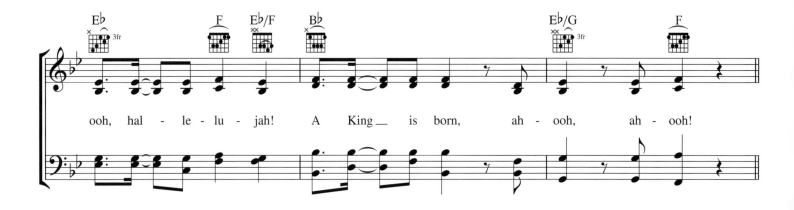

ooh, hal - le - lu - jah! A King __ is born, ah - ooh, ah - ooh!

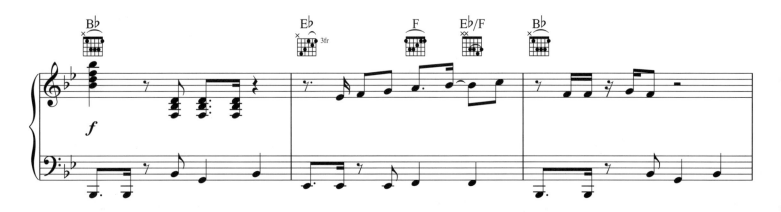

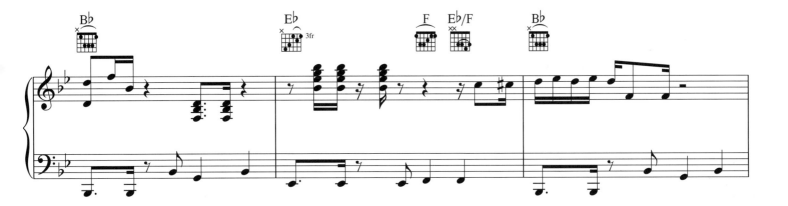

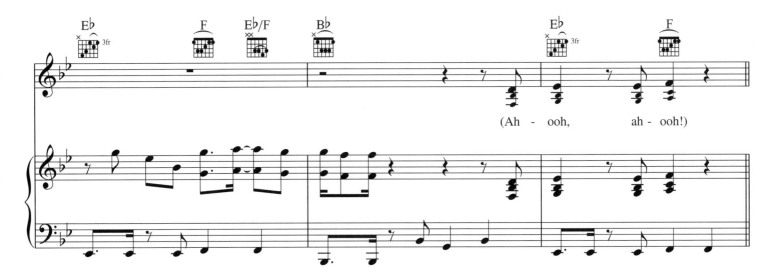

(Ah - ooh, ah - ooh!)

(Hal - le - lu - jah!) _____

A King __ is born this day __ in Beth - le - hem. __
pal - ace __ is low - ly, His throne __ is made of hay. __

His

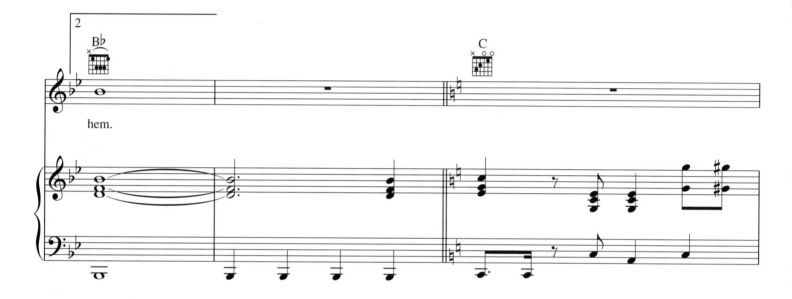

hem.

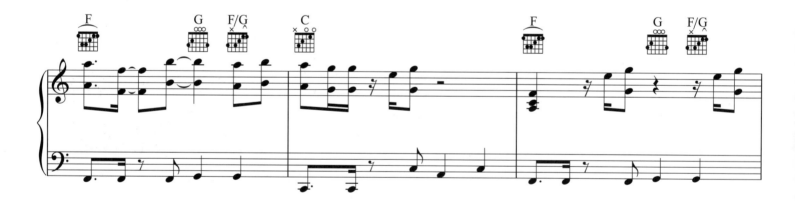

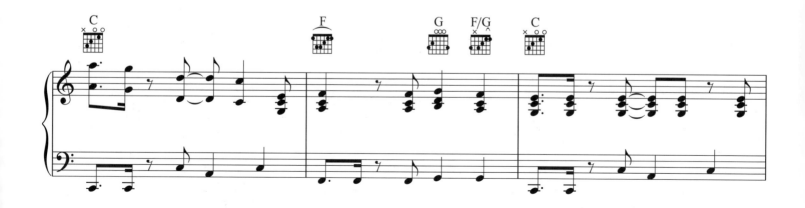

Come hum - bly and hum - bly bow; ___ He's
(Come hum - bly ___ and

in the man - ger now. _____ Come hum - bly and hum -
bow.)

- bly bow; ___ He's in the man - ger now. _____
(Come hum - bly ___ and bow.)

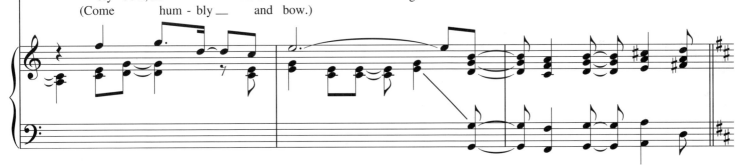

A King ___ is born this day ___ in Beth - le - hem. ___ (Hal - le - lu - jah! ___ Ah -

MANGER THRONE

Words and Music by
JULIE MILLER

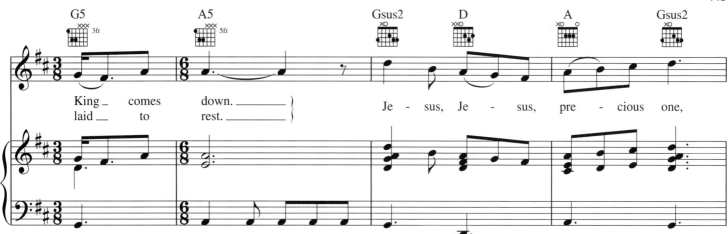

King __ comes down. ____ }
laid __ to rest. ____ }
Je - sus, Je - sus, pre - cious one,

How we thank You that __ You've __ come. Je - sus, Je - sus, pre - cious one; a

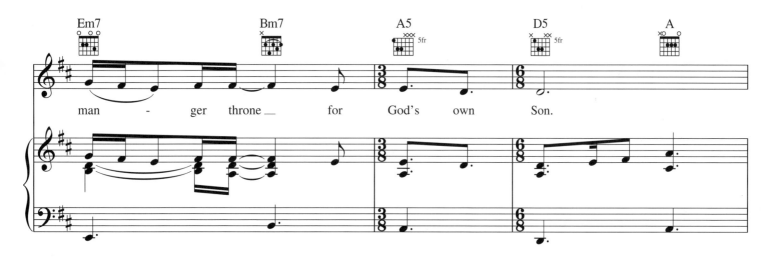

man - ger throne __ for God's own Son.

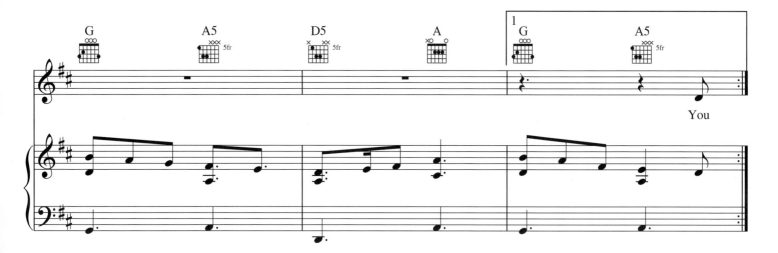

You

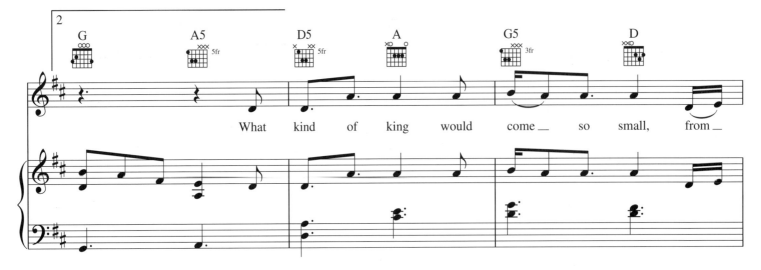

What kind of king would come __ so small, from __

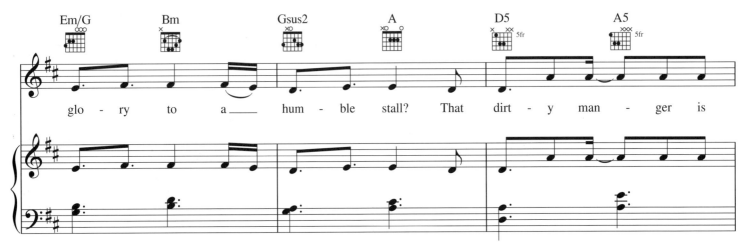

glo - ry to a ___ hum - ble stall? That dirt - y man - ger is

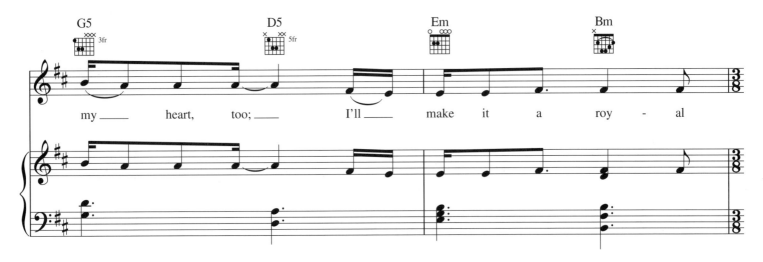

my ___ heart, too; ___ I'll ___ make it a roy - al

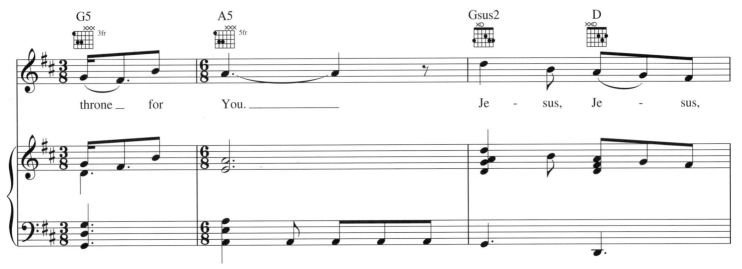

throne __ for You. _____ Je - sus, Je - sus,

pre - cious one; how we thank You that You've ___ come. ___

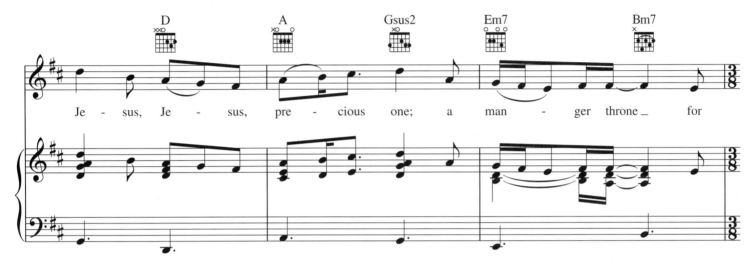

Je - sus, Je - sus, pre - cious one; a man - ger throne ___ for

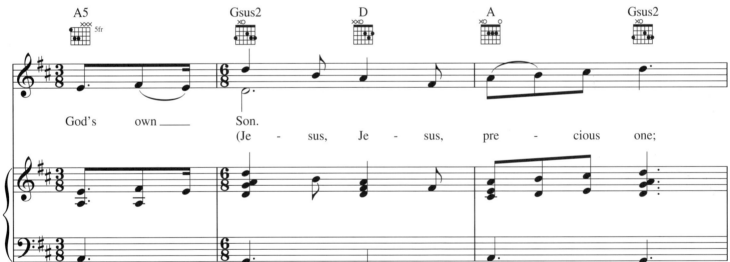

God's own ___ Son. (Je - sus, Je - sus, pre - cious one;

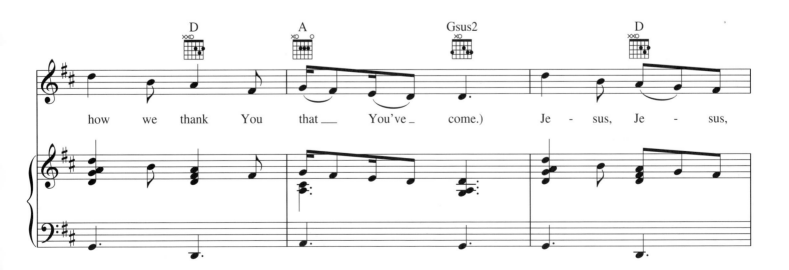

how we thank You that ___ You've ___ come.) Je - sus, Je - sus,

pre - cious one; a man - ger throne, __ (My heart __ is a throne,) my

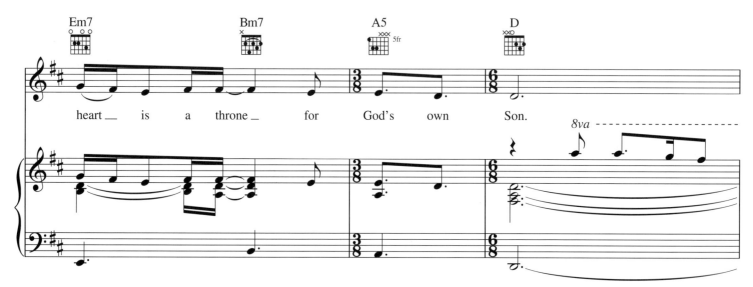

heart __ is a throne __ for God's own Son.

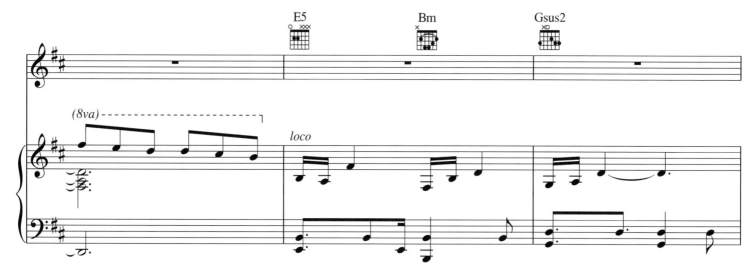

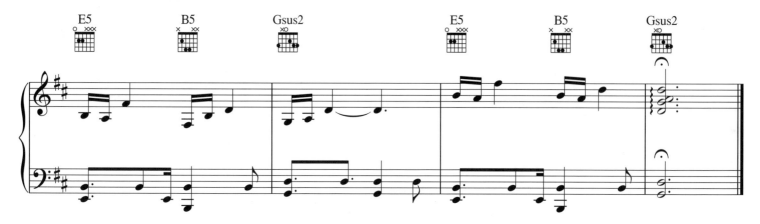

NOT THAT FAR FROM BETHLEHEM

Words and Music by JEFF BORDERS,
GAYLA BORDERS and LOWELL ALEXANDER

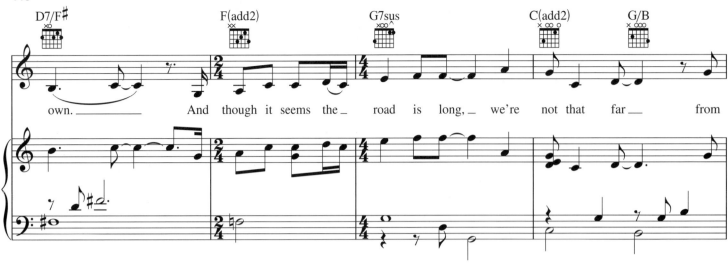

own. _____ And though it seems the _ road is long, _ we're not that far _ from

Beth - le - hem, _____ where all our hope _ and joy be - gin. _ For _____

in our arms, _ we'll cher - ish Him. _____ We're not that far _____

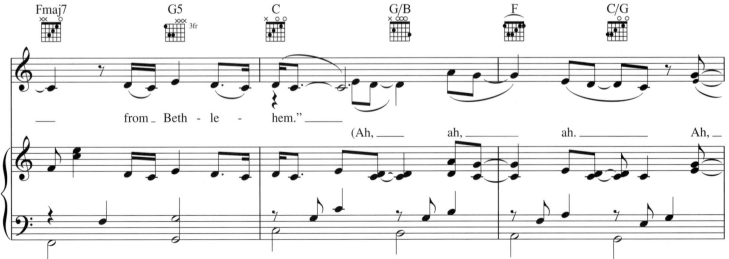

_ from _ Beth - le - hem." _____

(Ah, ____ ah, _____ ah. _____ Ah, _

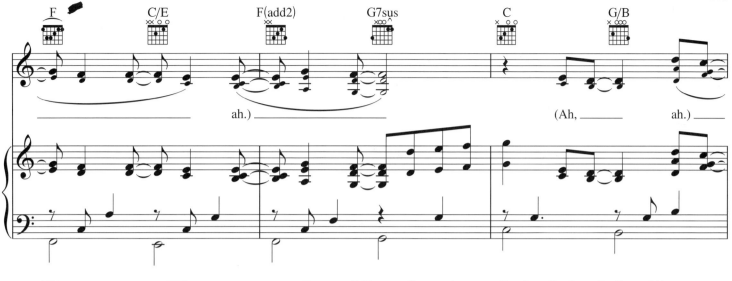

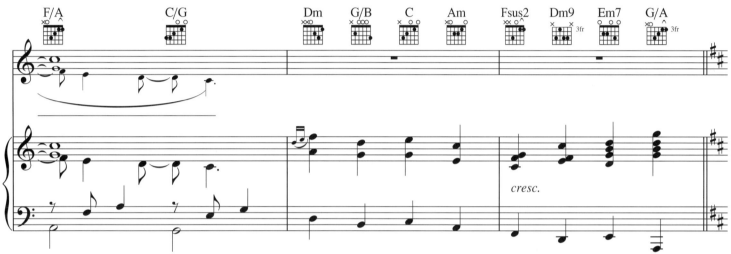

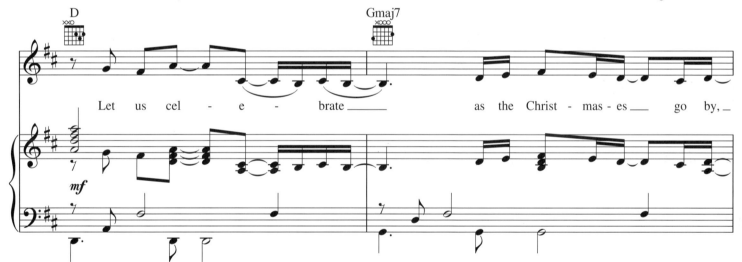

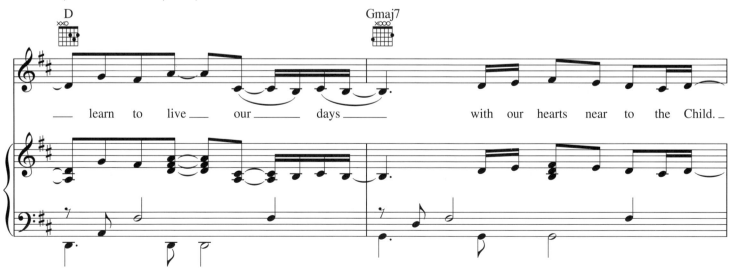

Ever drawn, ever close to the only love that
(Ev-er drawn, ev-er close.)

lasts. And though two thou-sand years have passed, we're

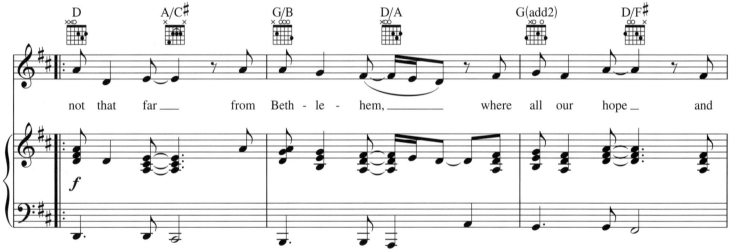

not that far from Beth-le-hem, where all our hope and

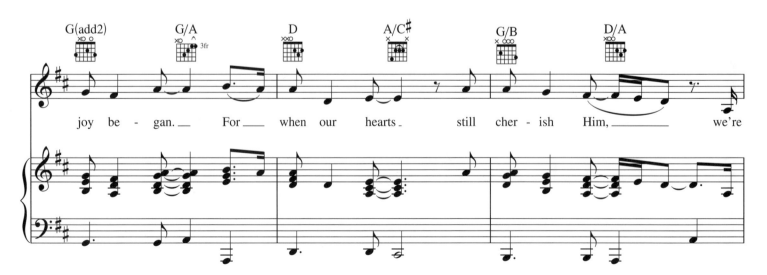

joy be-gan. For when our hearts still cher-ish Him, we're

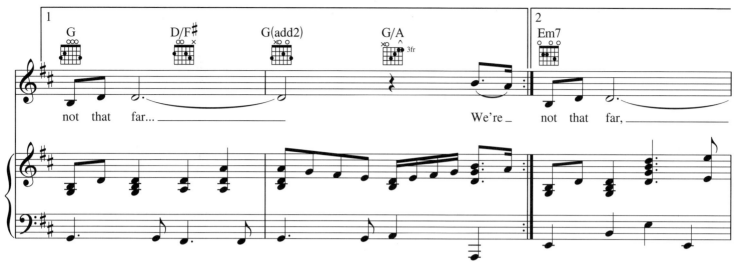

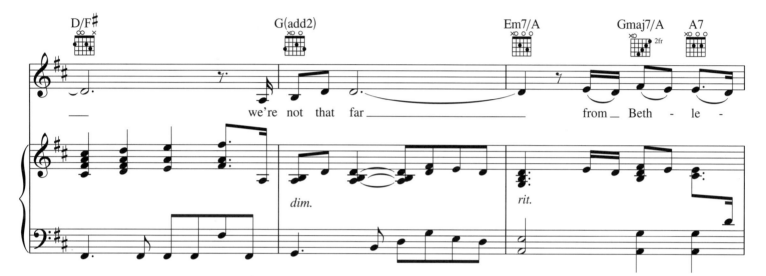

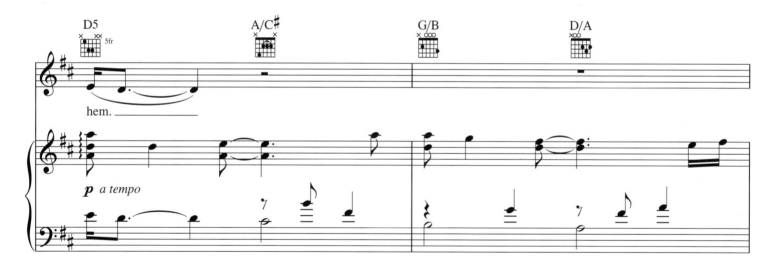

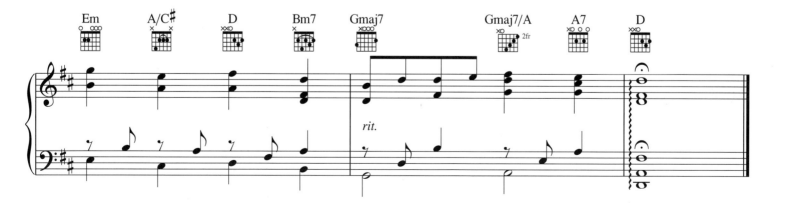

O COME, ALL YE FAITHFUL

Words and Music by REBECCA ST. JAMES
and TEDD TJORNHOM

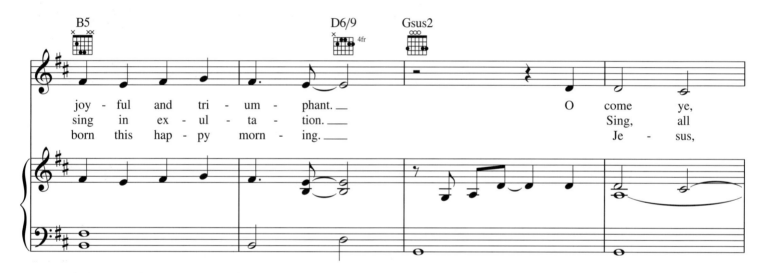

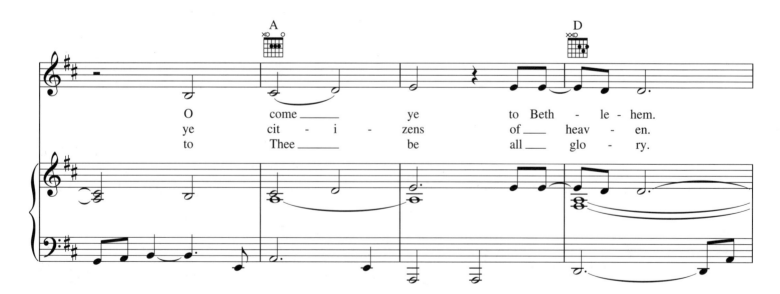

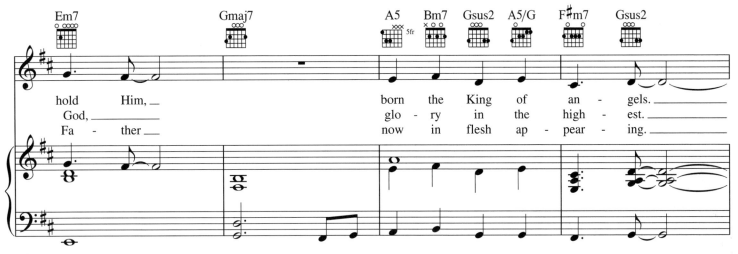

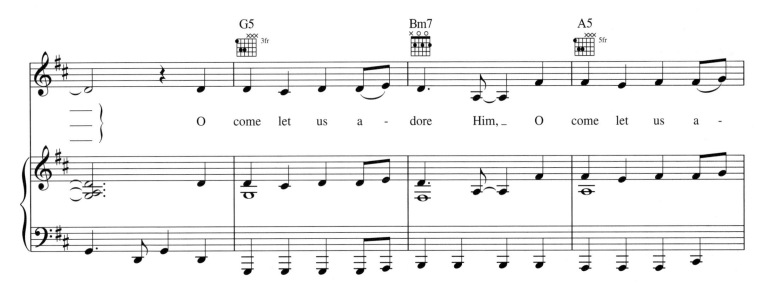

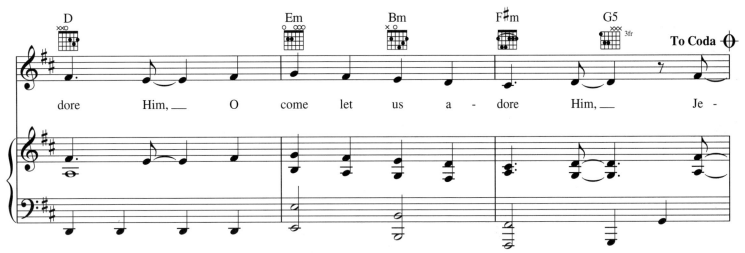

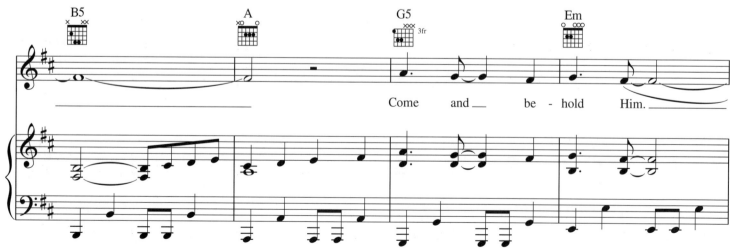

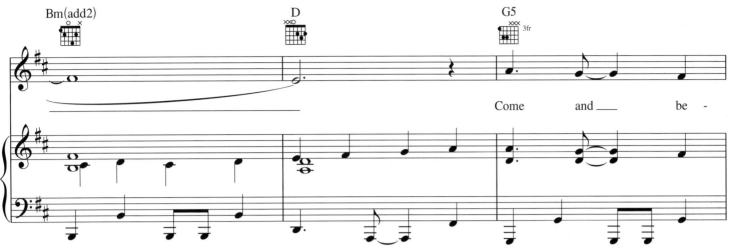

Come and ___ be -

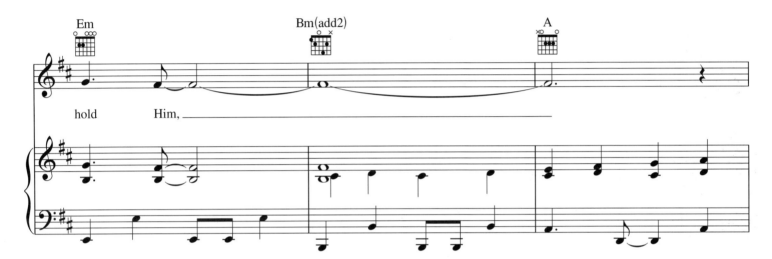

hold Him, _____

born the King of an - gels. _____

D.S. al Coda

CODA

- sus. _____ O come let us a -

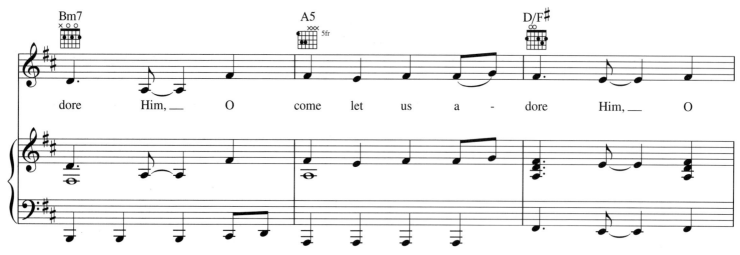

dore Him, __ O come let us a - dore Him, __ O

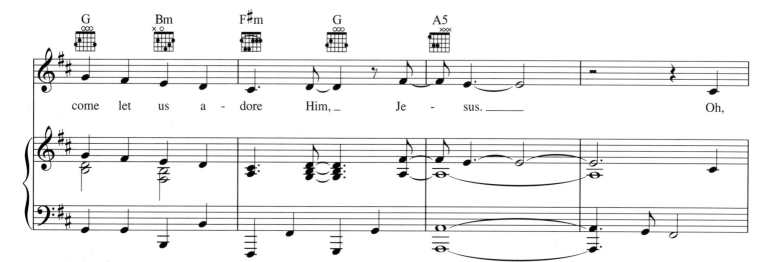

come let us a - dore Him, _ Je - sus. _____ Oh,

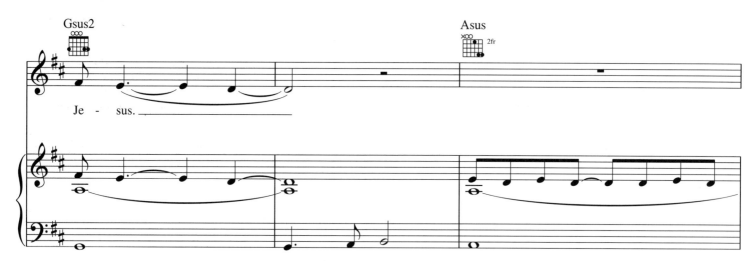

Je - sus. _____

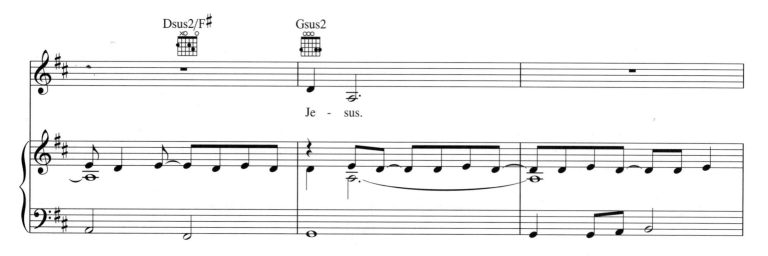

Je - sus.

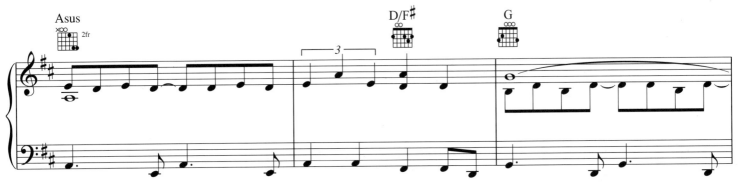

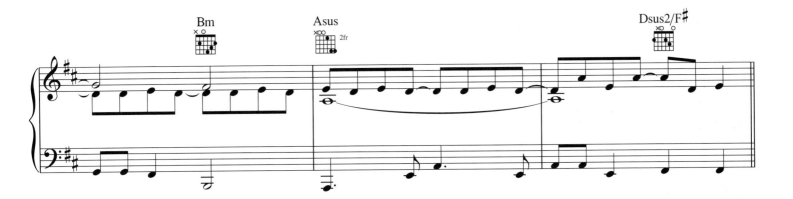

(Let us ___ a - dore.) ___

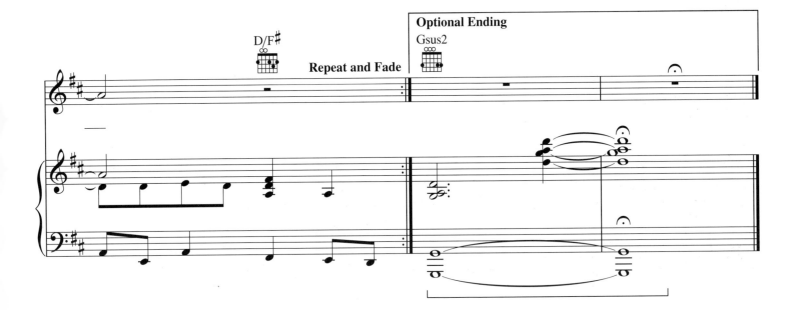

Optional Ending

Repeat and Fade

ONE KING

Words and Music by JEFF BORDERS,
GAYLA BORDERS and LOWELL ALEXANDER

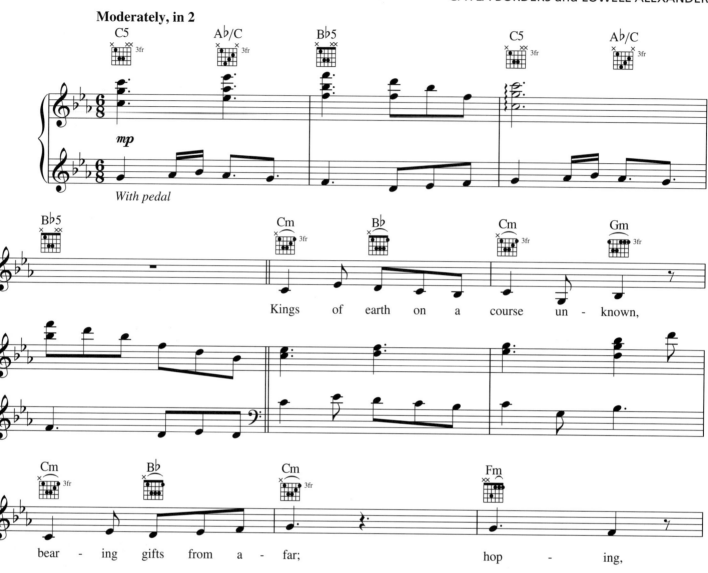

Moderately, in 2

mp

With pedal

Kings of earth on a course un-known, bear-ing gifts from a-far; hop-ing, pray-ing, fol-low-ing yon-der star.

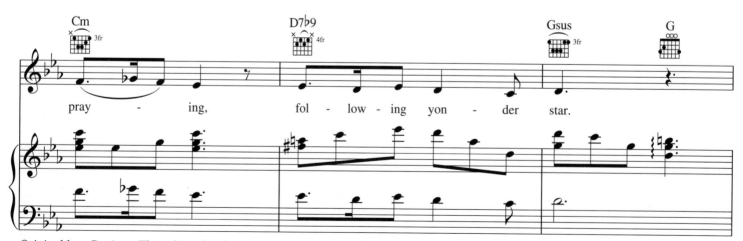

Original key: B minor. This edition has been transposed up one half-step to be more playable.

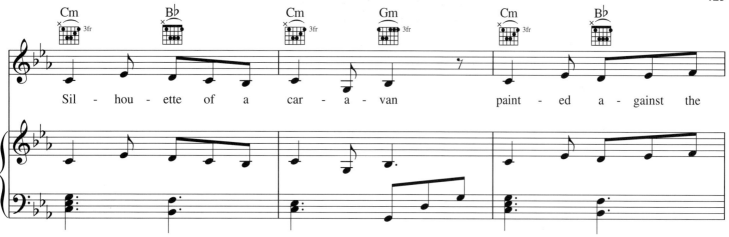

Sil - hou - ette of a car - a - van paint - ed a - gainst the

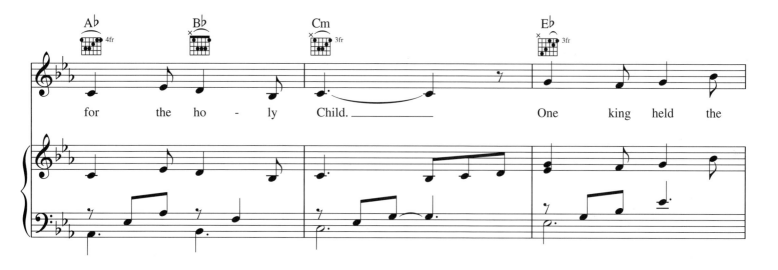

sky; _____ wise men search - ing

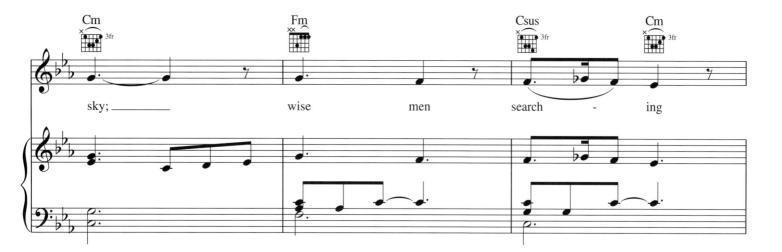

for the ho - ly Child. _____ One king held the

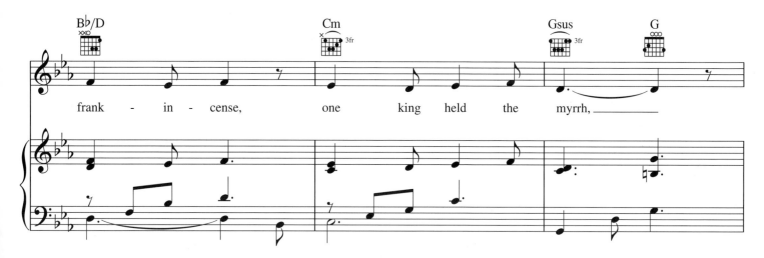

frank - in - cense, one king held the myrrh, _____

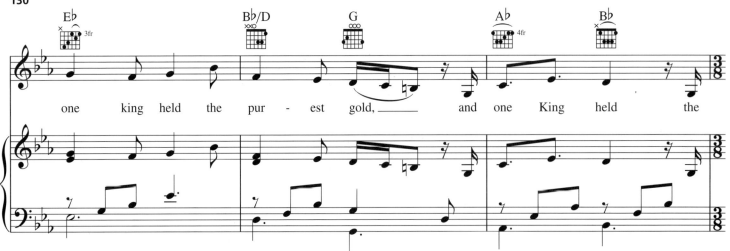

one king held the pur - est gold, ____ and one King held the

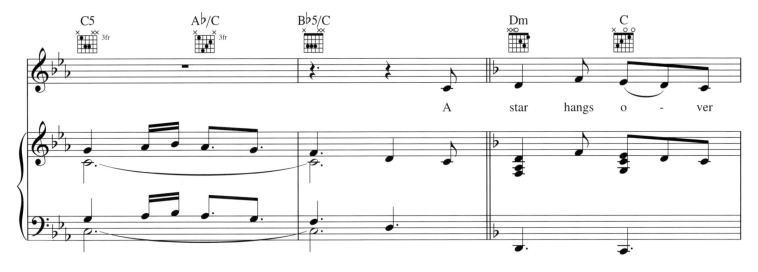

hope of the world.

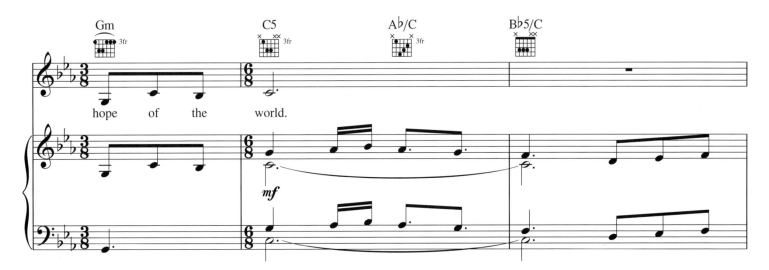

A star hangs o - ver

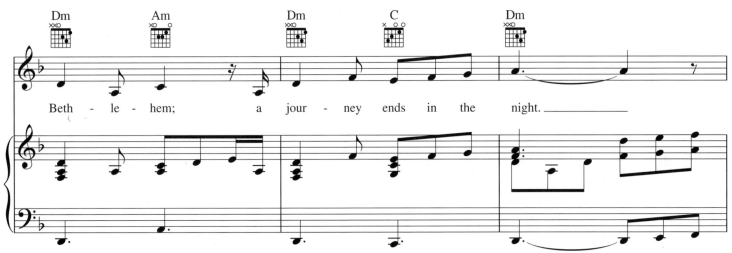

Beth - le - hem; a jour - ney ends in the night. ____

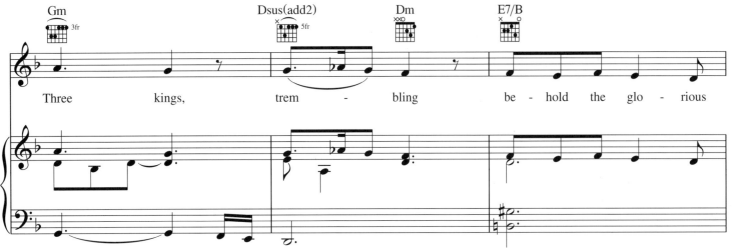

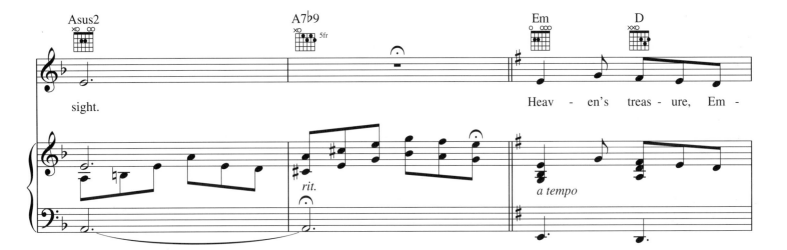

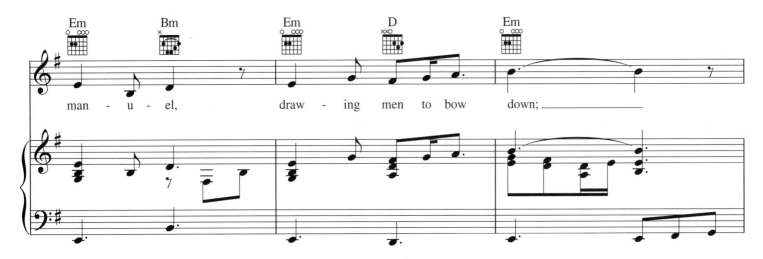

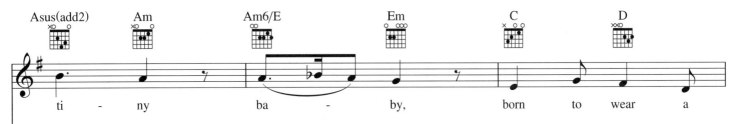

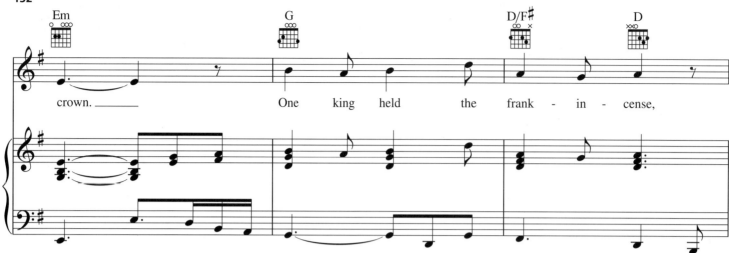

crown. _____ One king held the frank - in - cense,

One king held the myrrh, _____ one king held the

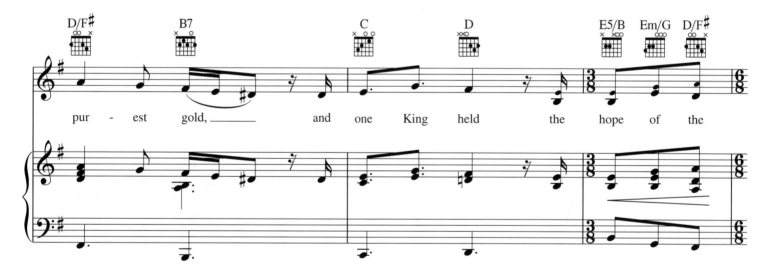

pur - est gold, _____ and one King held the hope of the

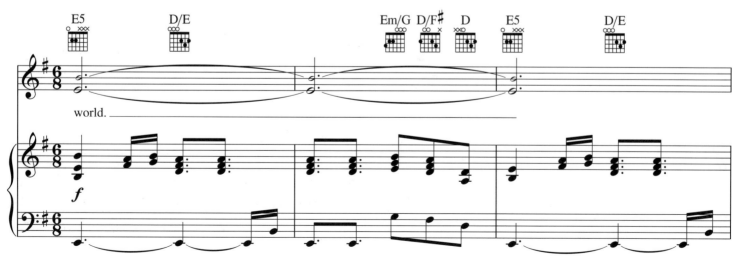

world. _____

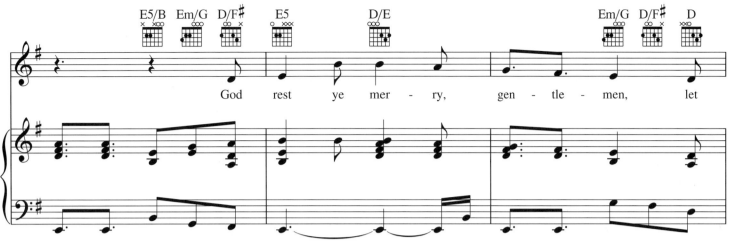

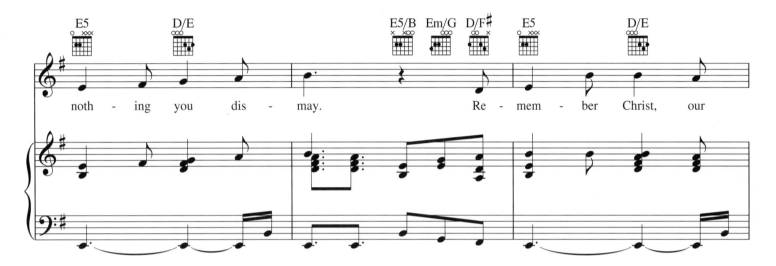

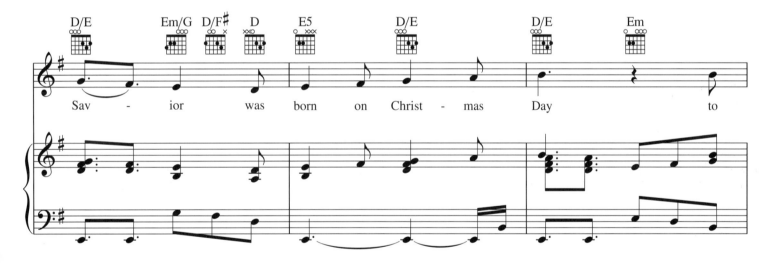

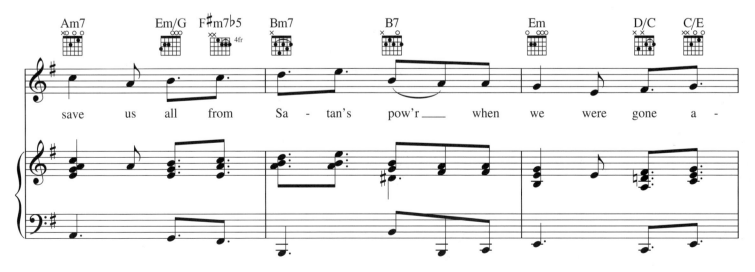

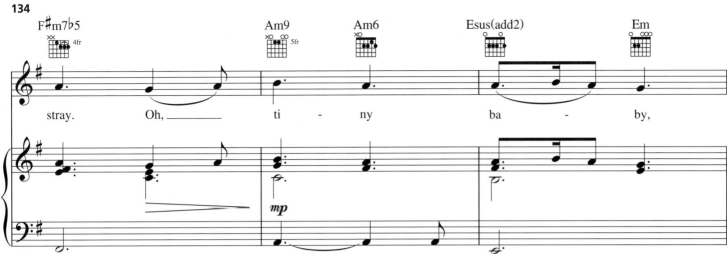

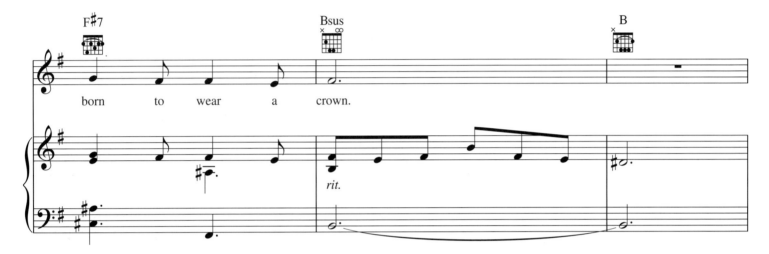

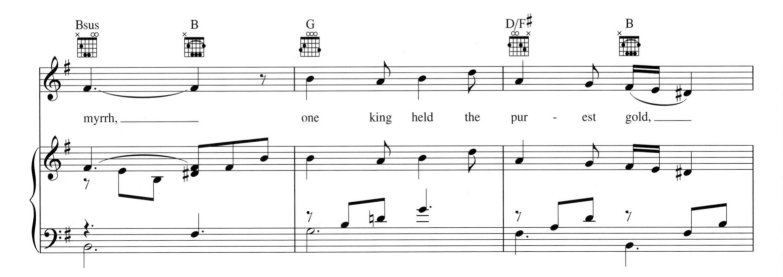

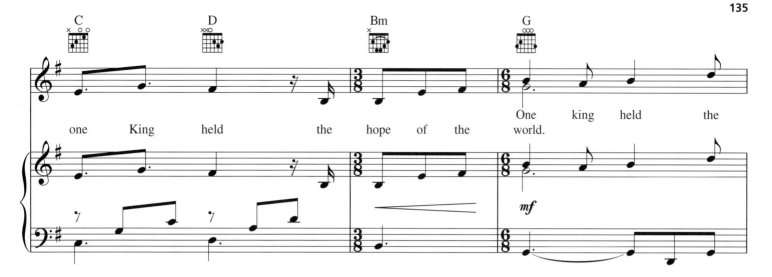

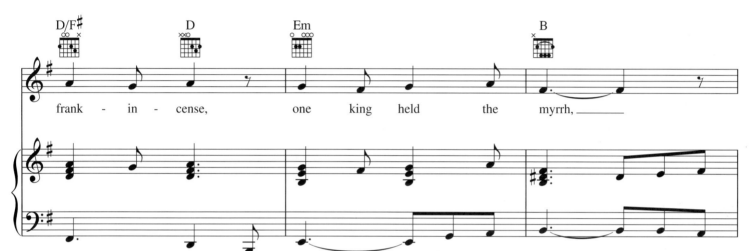

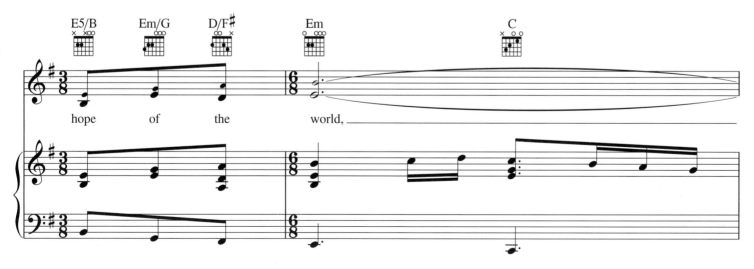

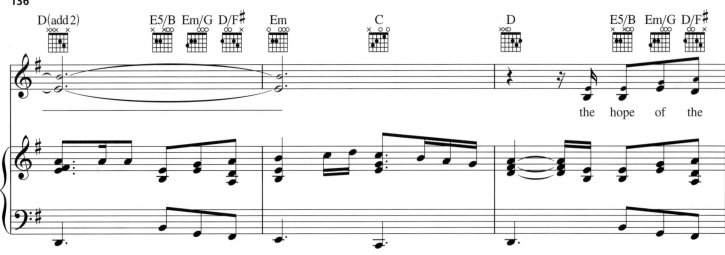

the hope of the

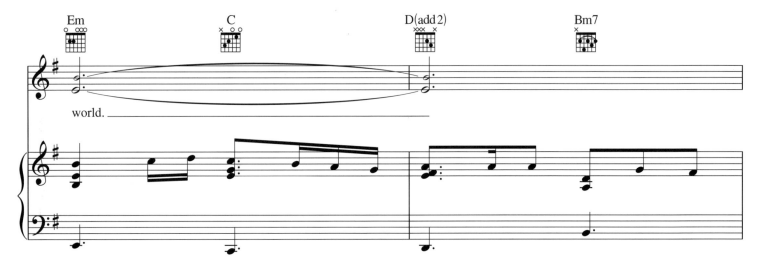

world. _____

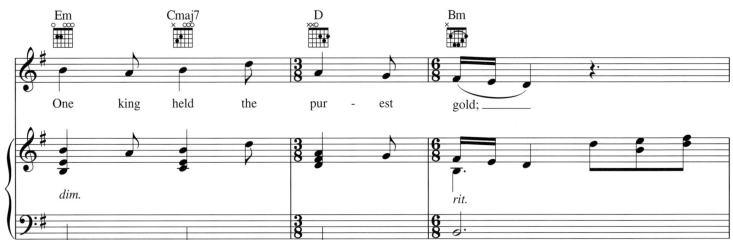

One king held the pur - est gold; _____

dim.   rit.

one king held the hope of the world.

mp   molto rit.

PERFECT LOVE
(Mary's Song)

Words and Music by RUSSELL FRAGAR
and DARLENE ZSCHECH

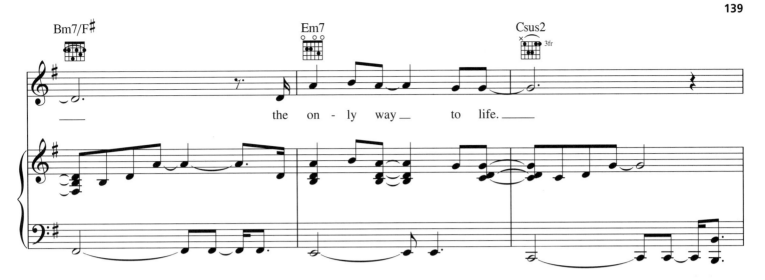

the on-ly way__ to life. ___

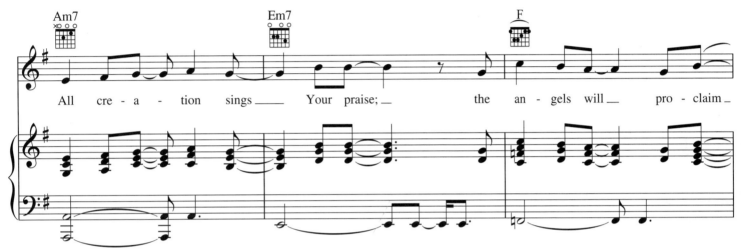

All cre-a-tion sings ___ Your praise; ___ the an-gels will __ pro-claim __

my pre-cious Je - sus. ____

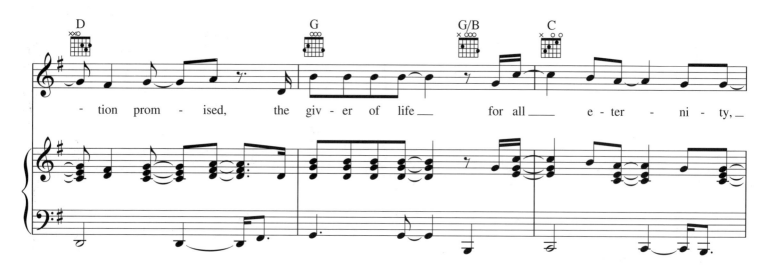

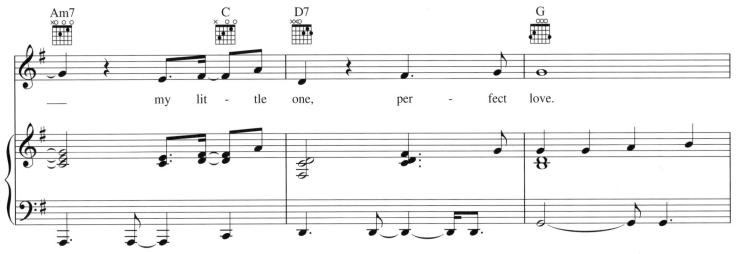

my lit - tle one, per - fect love.

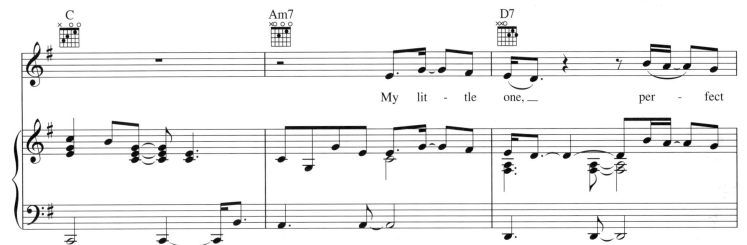

My lit - tle one, ___ per - fect

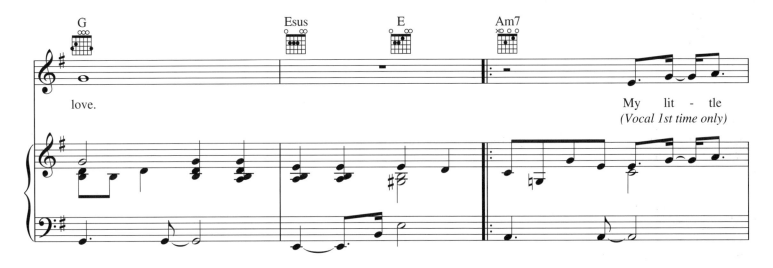

love. My lit - tle
(Vocal 1st time only)

Repeat and Fade   **Optional Ending**

G(add2)

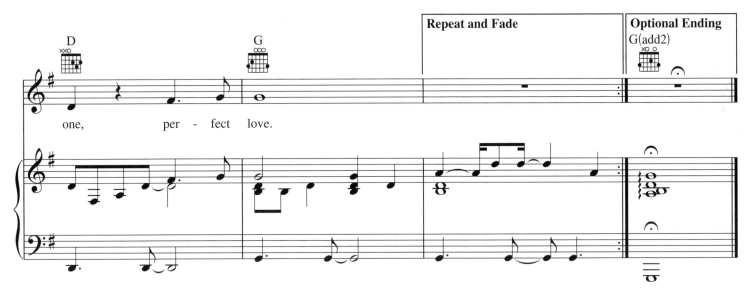

one, per - fect love.

OUR GOD IS WITH US

Words and Music by STEVEN CURTIS CHAPMAN
and MICHAEL W. SMITH

Freely

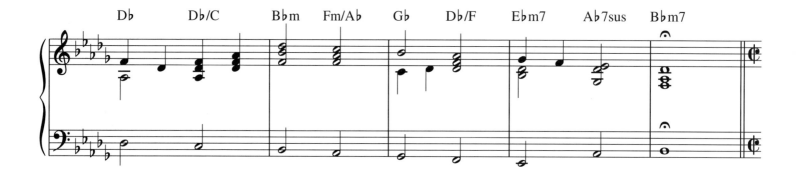

With motion

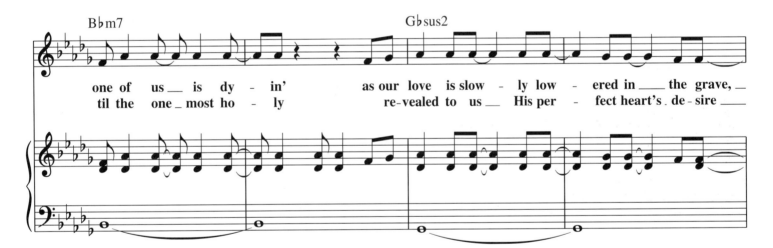

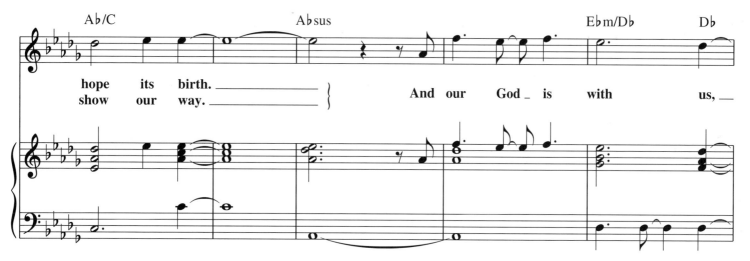

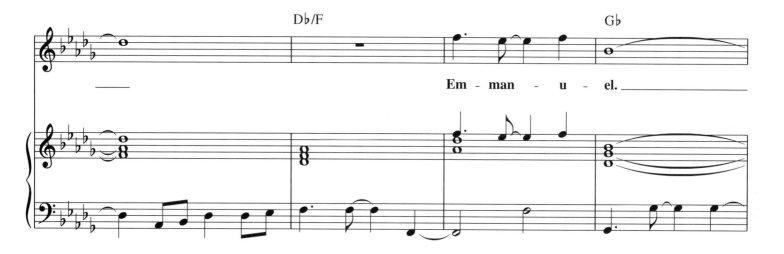

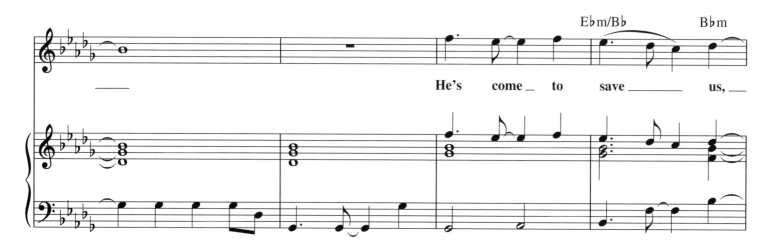

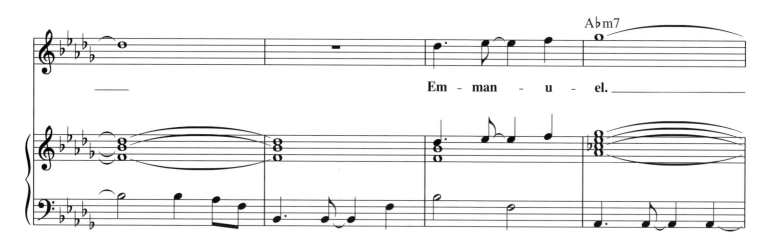

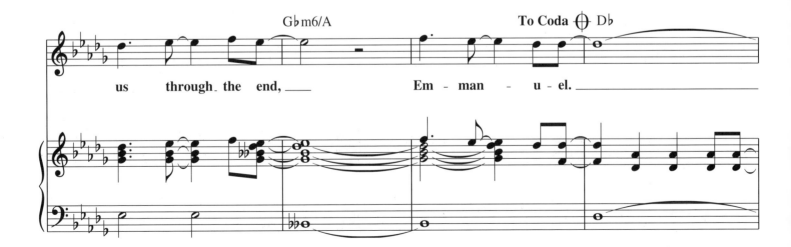

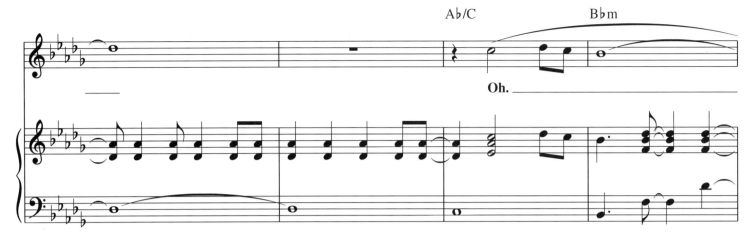

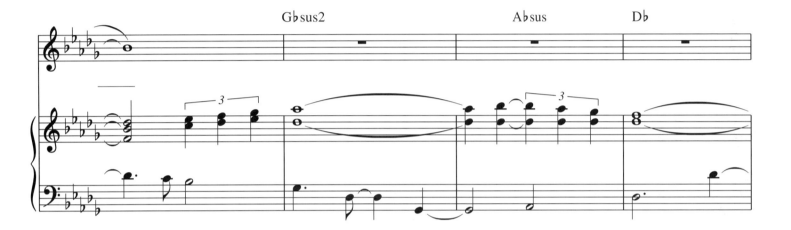

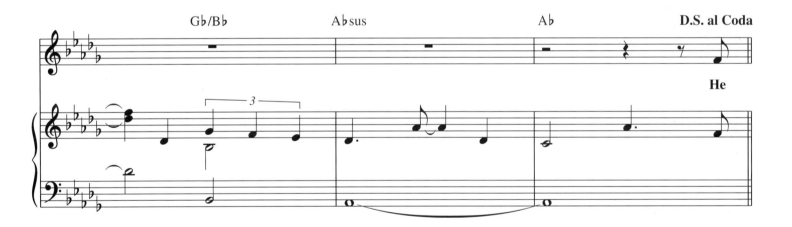

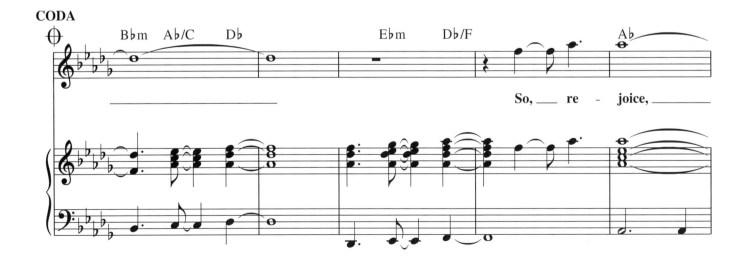

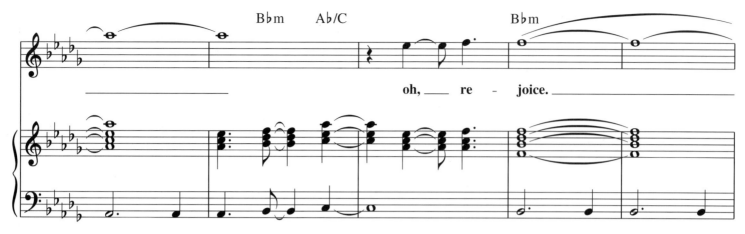

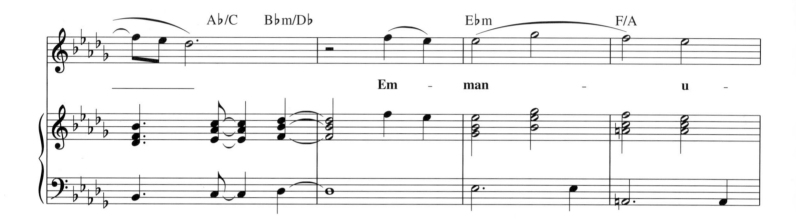

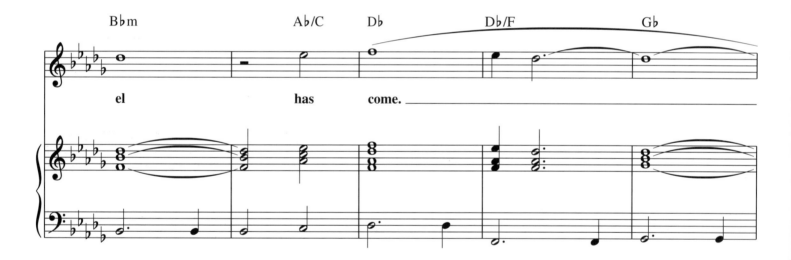

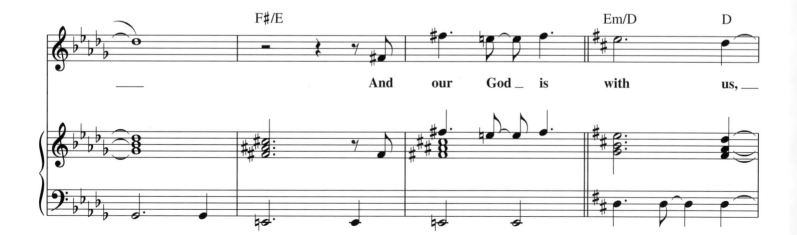

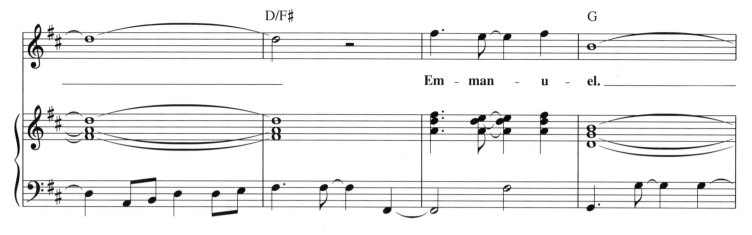

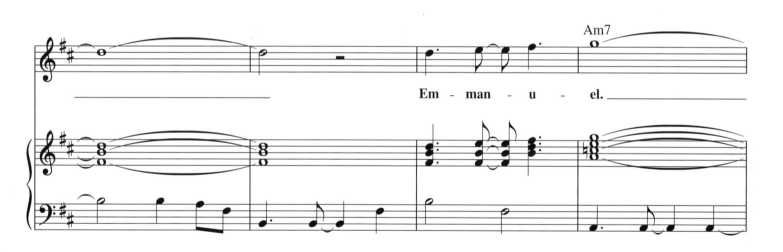

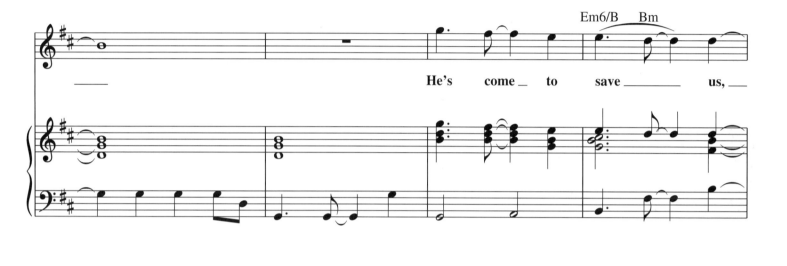

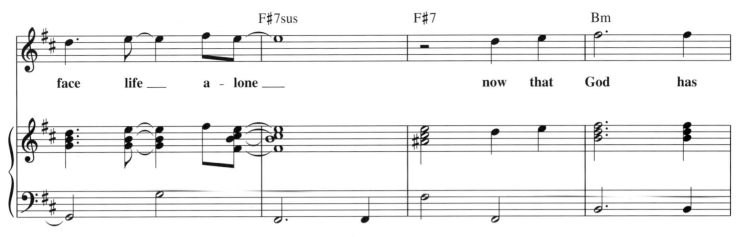

face life ___ a - lone ___ now that God has

made him - self known _____ as Fa - ther _ and friend, with

us to the end, Em - man - u - el. _____

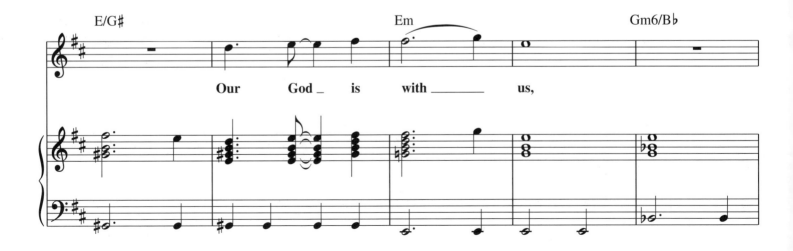

Our God _ is with _____ us,

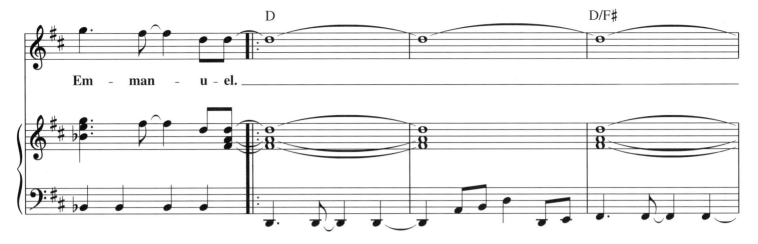

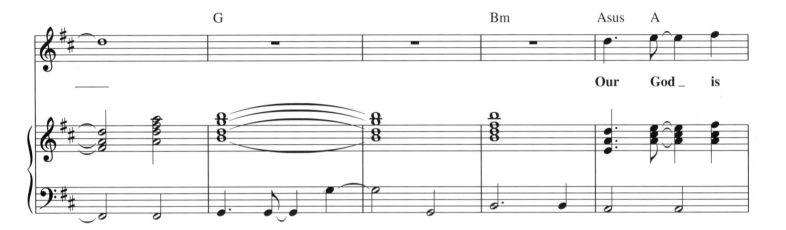

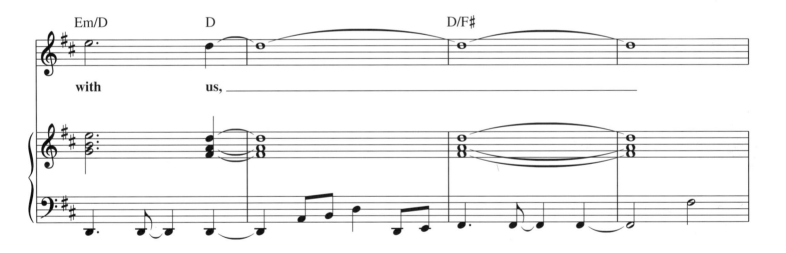

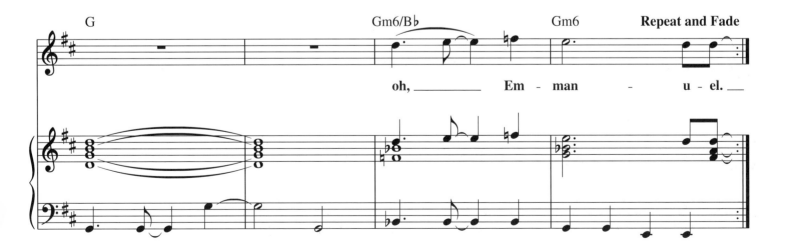

PRECIOUS PROMISE

Words and Music by
STEVEN CURTIS CHAPMAN

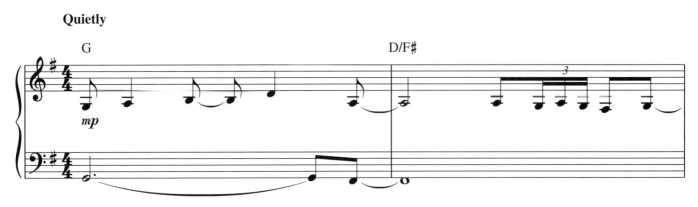

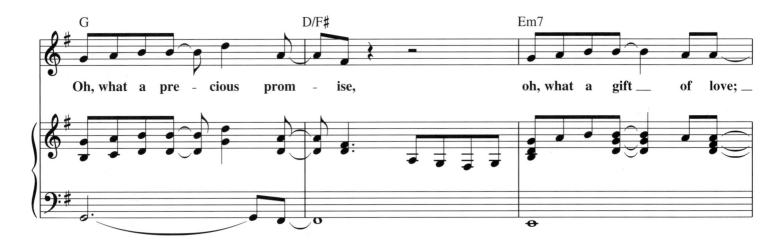

Oh, what a pre- cious prom- ise, oh, what a gift __ of love; __

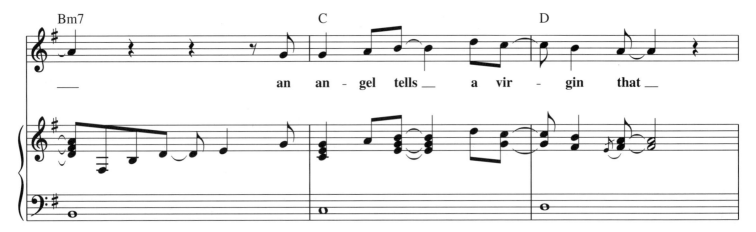

__ an an- gel tells __ a vir- gin that __

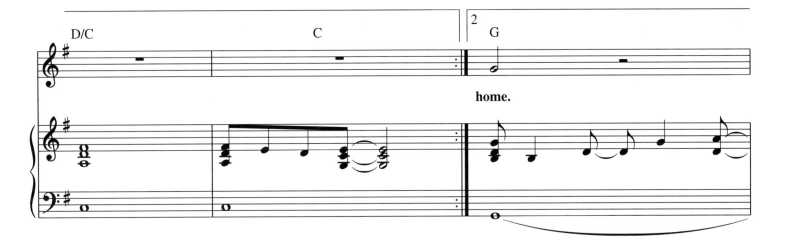

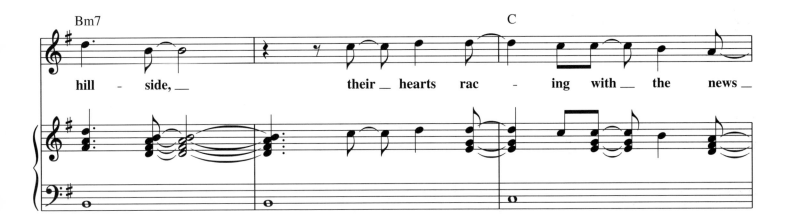

the an - gel told them. ___

A

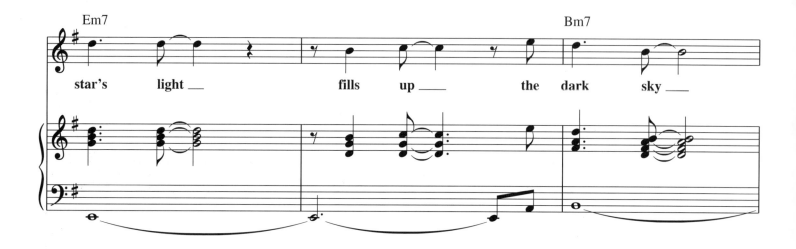

star's light ___ fills up ___ the dark sky ___

as the night of pre - cious prom - ise is un -

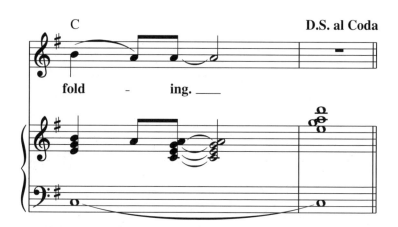

fold - ing. ___

D.S. al Coda

CODA

man - ger in Beth - le - hem.

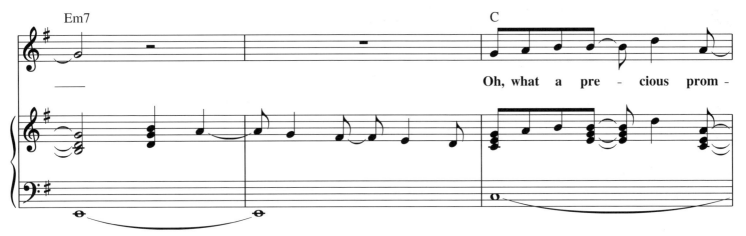

Oh, what a pre - cious prom -

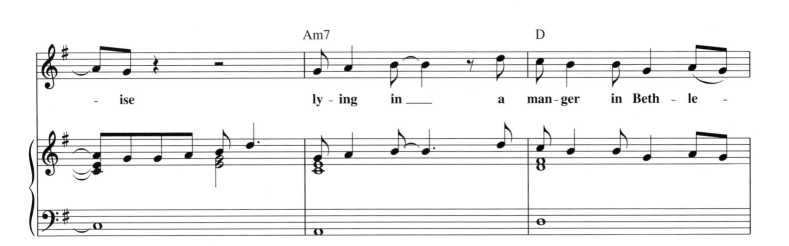

- ise ly - ing in ___ a man - ger in Beth - le -

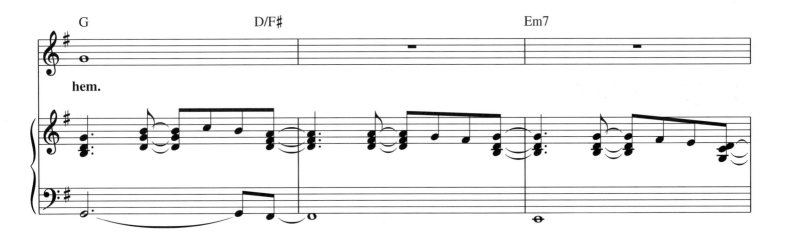

hem.

ROSE OF BETHLEHEM

Words and Music by
LOWELL ALEXANDER

161

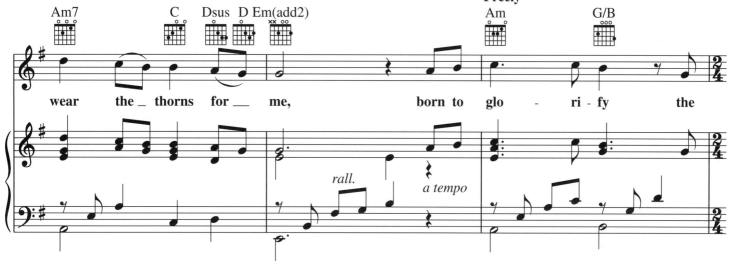

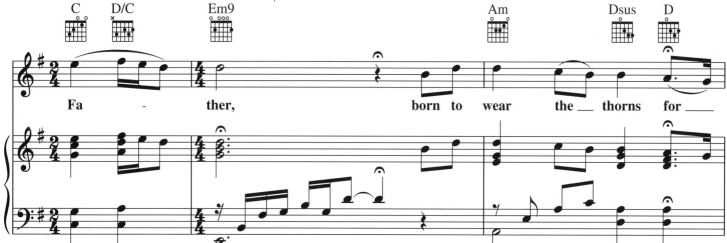

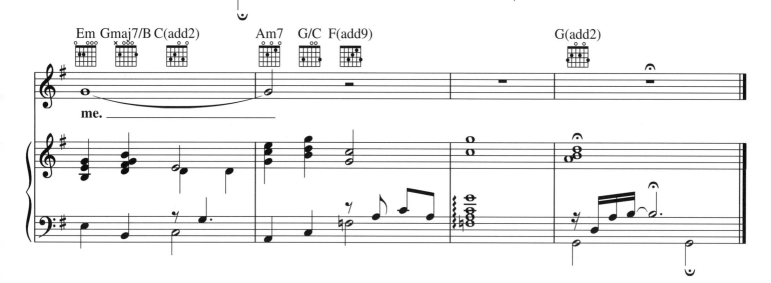

SEASON OF LOVE

Words and Music by HUNTER DAVIS,
GEORGE COCCHINI and CHRIS FAULK

Slow half-time feel

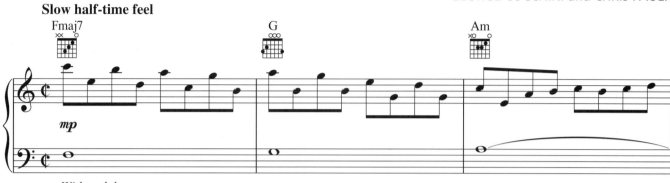

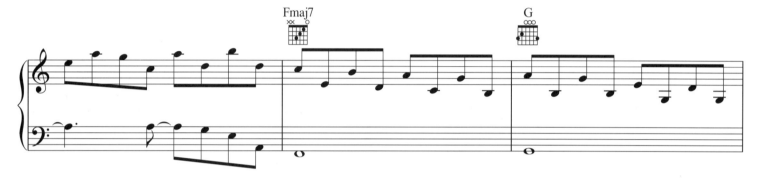

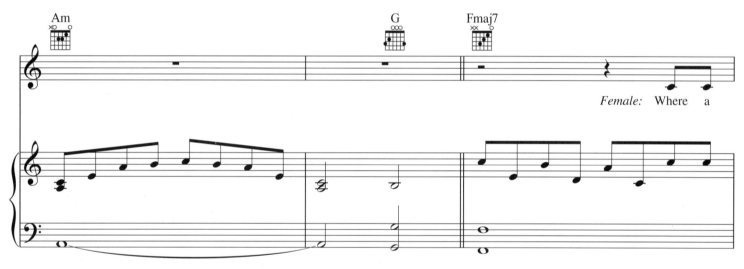

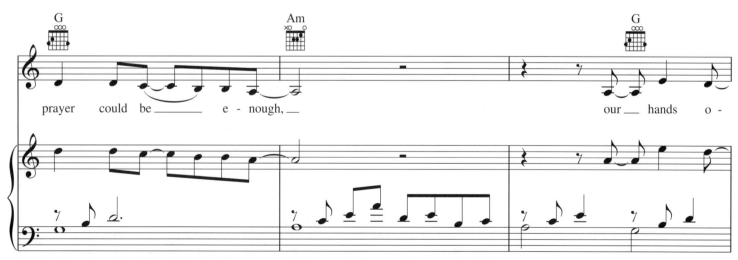

Original key: B major. This edition has been transposed up one half-step to be more playable.

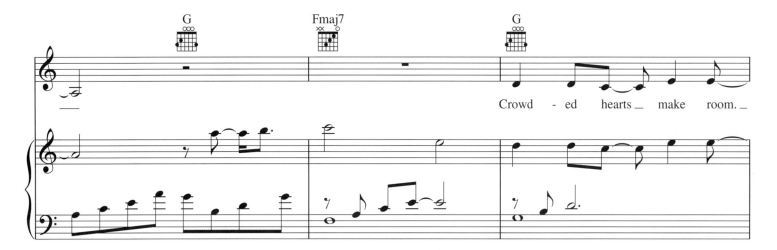

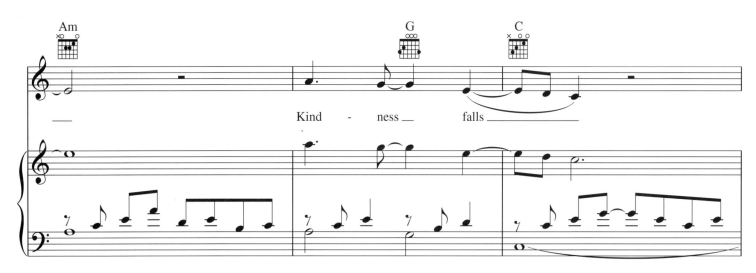

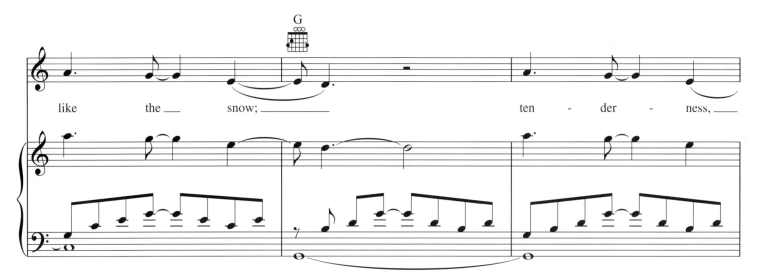

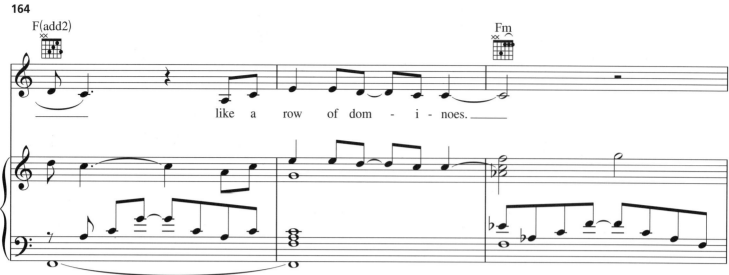

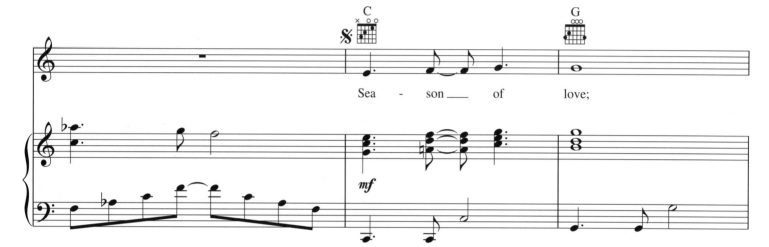

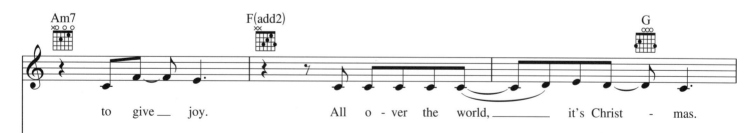

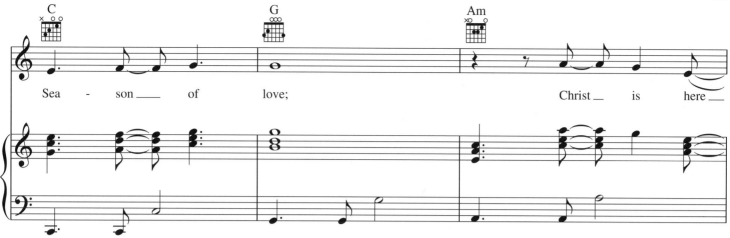

Sea - son ___ of love; Christ ___ is here ___

___ with ___ us, in our ___ hearts, through our ___ hands.

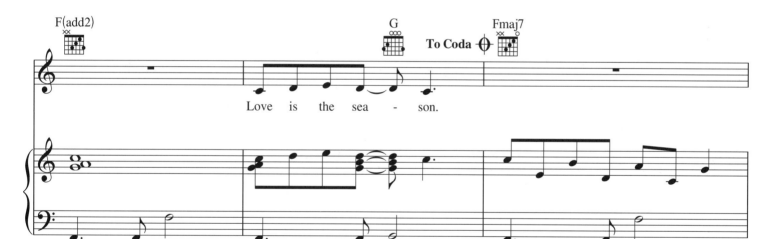

To Coda

Love is the sea - son.

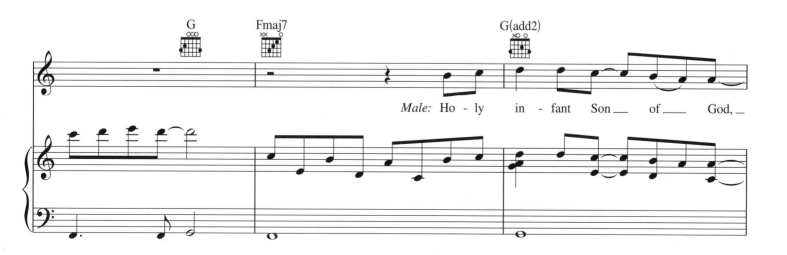

Male: Ho - ly in - fant Son ___ of ___ God, ___

You are ___ the light ___ in - side ___

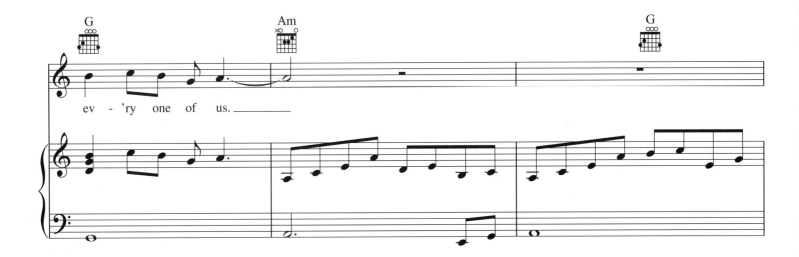

ev - 'ry one of us. ___

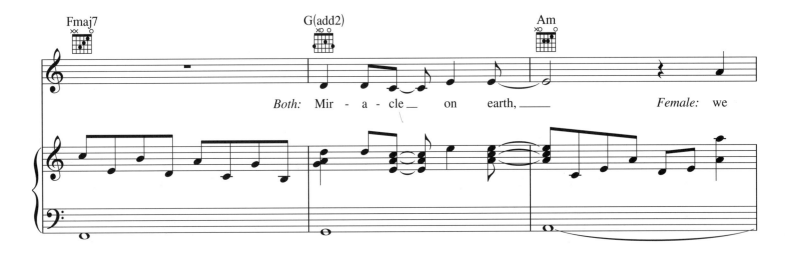

Both: Mir - a - cle ___ on earth, ___ *Female:* we

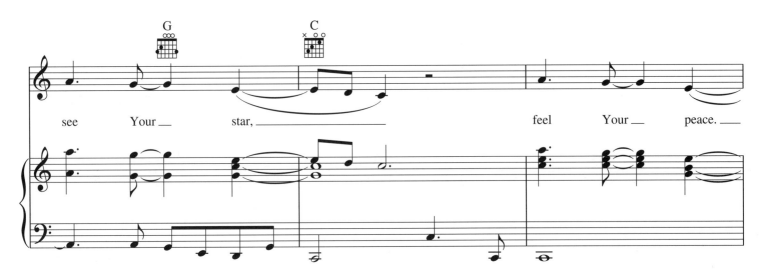

see Your ___ star, ___ feel Your ___ peace. ___

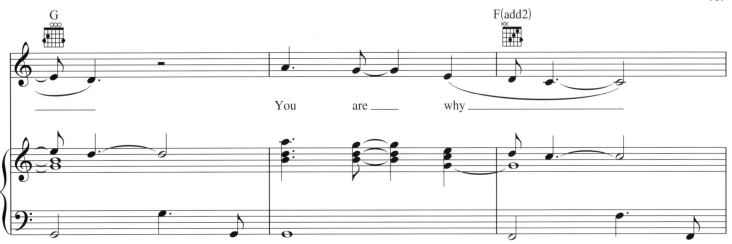

You are ___ why ___

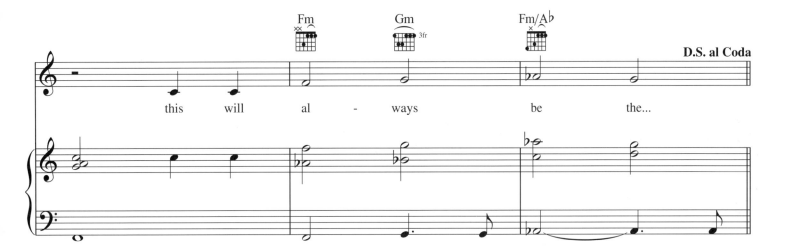

D.S. al Coda

this will al - ways be the...

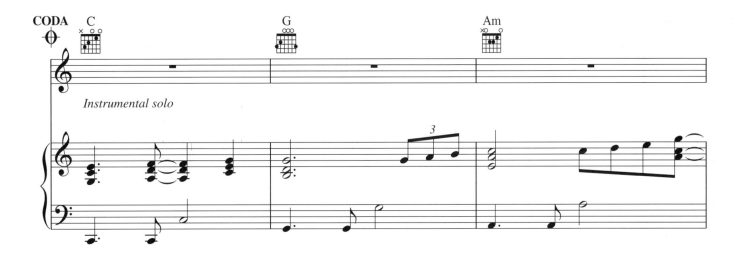

CODA

Instrumental solo

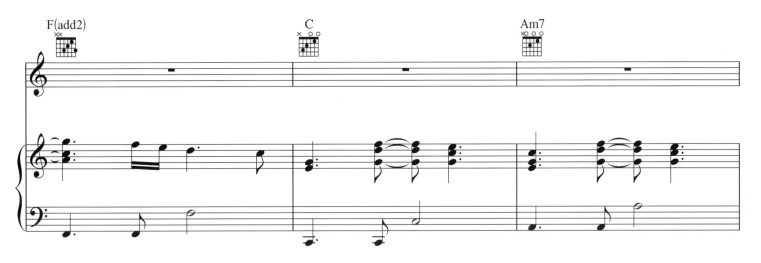

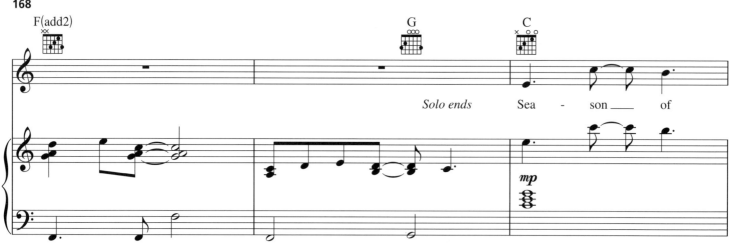

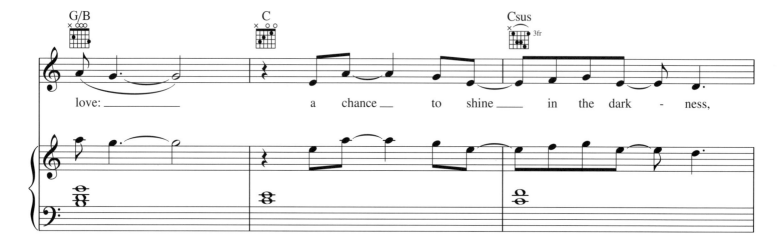

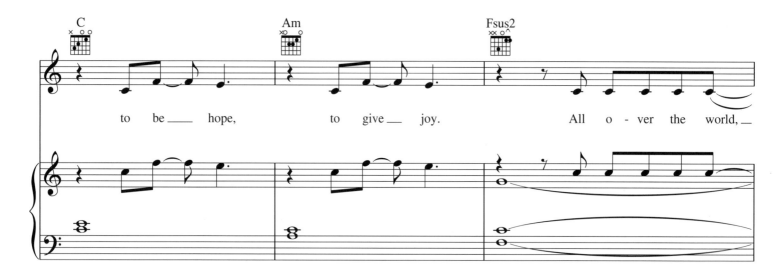

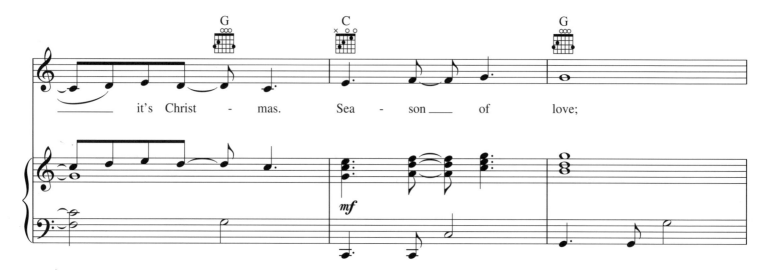

Christ ___ is here _____ with ___ us, in our ___ hearts,

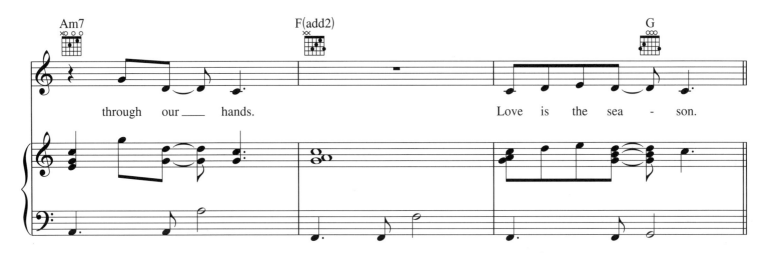

through our ___ hands. Love is the sea - son.

Vocal ad lib.

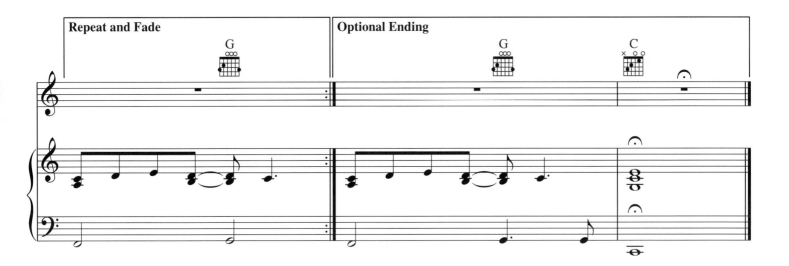

Repeat and Fade

Optional Ending

A STRANGE WAY TO SAVE THE WORLD

Words and Music by DAVE CLARK,
MARK HARRIS and DON KOCH

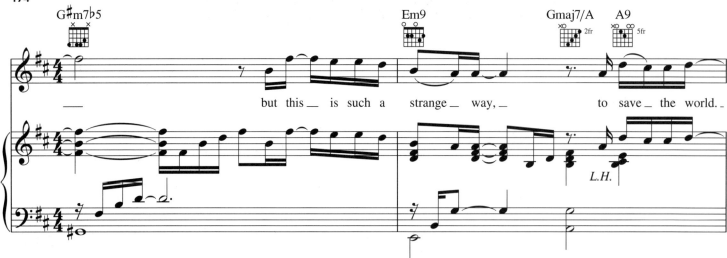

but this — is such a strange — way, — to save — the world. —

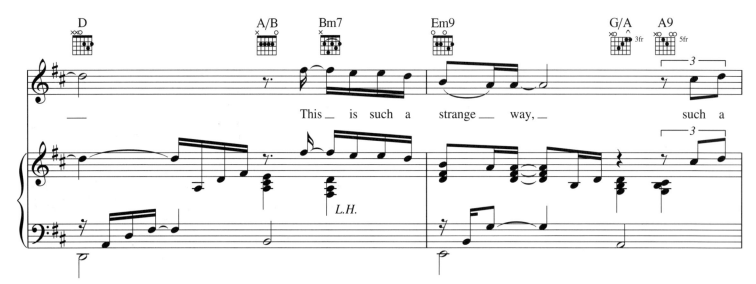

This — is such a strange — way, — such a

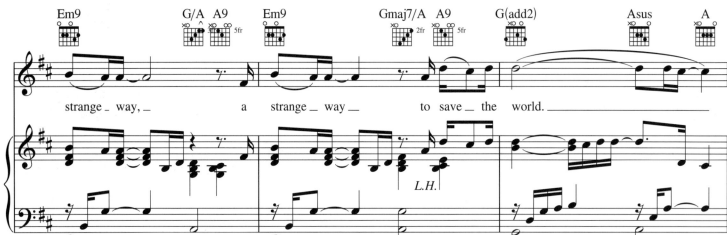

strange — way, — a strange — way — to save — the world. ____

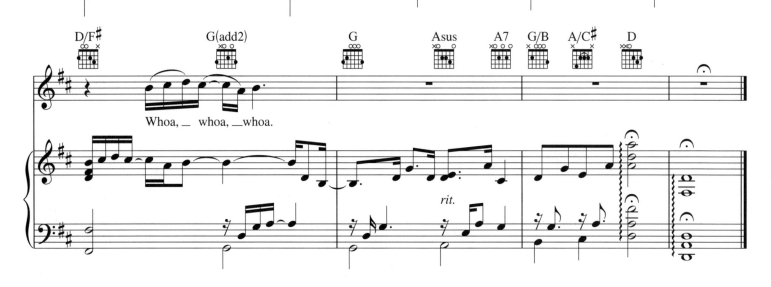

Whoa, — whoa, — whoa.

YOU ARE EMMANUEL

Words and Music by PAUL BALOCHE
and CLAIRE CLONINGER

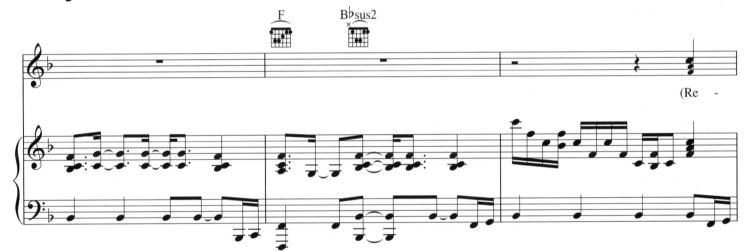

(Re -

joice,   re - joice,   re - joice,   Em man -
(Re - joice,   re - joice!)

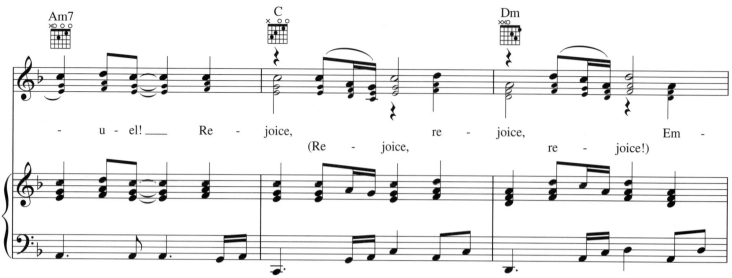

- u - el! __ Re - joice, re - joice, Em -
(Re - joice, re - joice!)

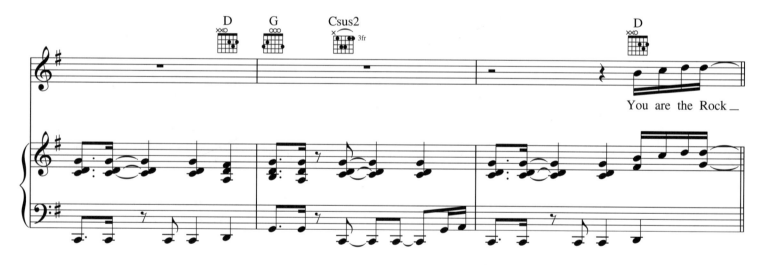

man - u - el!) _____

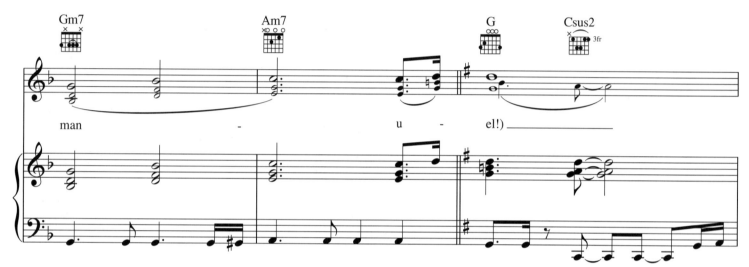

You are the Rock __

__ that will __ not fall; __ You are the God __ a - bove __ us all. ___ Oh __
__ and morn - ing star; __ You are the heal - er of __ our hearts. __ Oh __

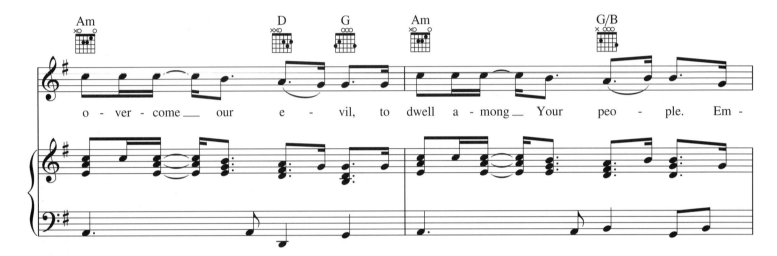

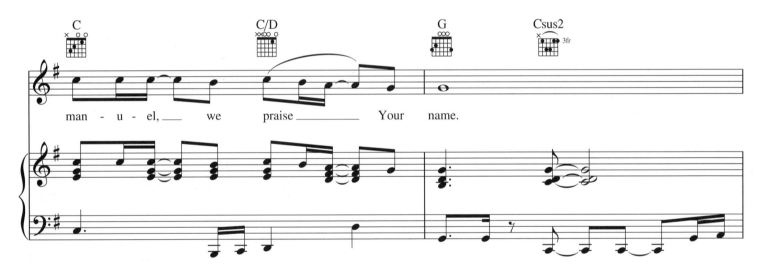

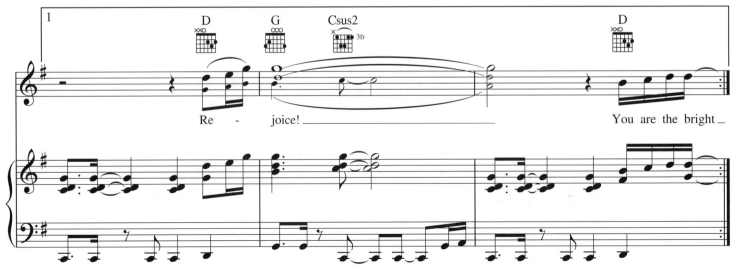

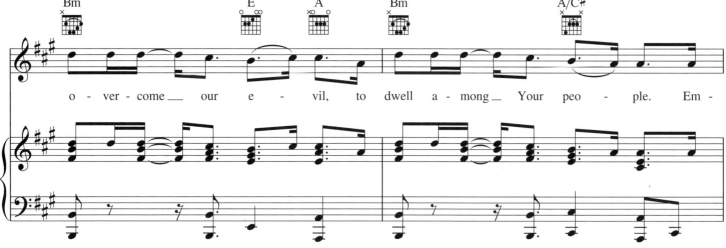

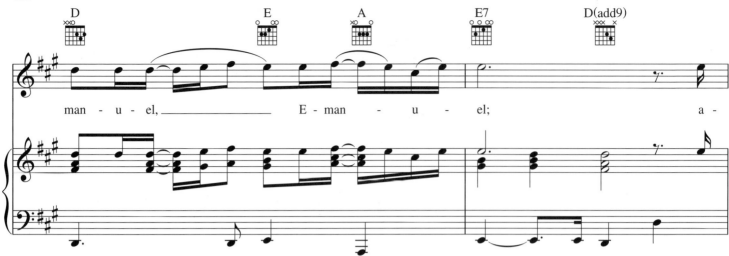

man - u - el, _____ E - man - u - el; _____ a -

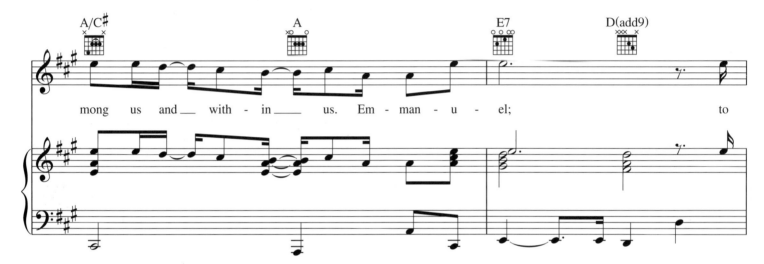

mong us and __ with - in __ us. Em - man - u - el; _____ to

earth you free - ly came, __ to o - ver - come __ our e - vil, to

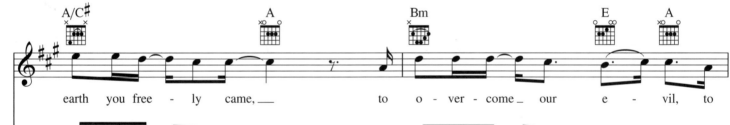

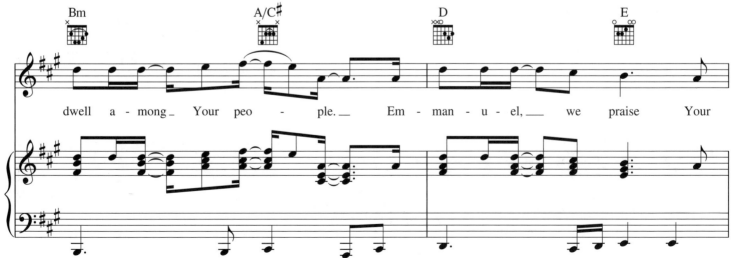

dwell a - mong __ Your peo - ple. __ Em - man - u - el, __ we praise Your

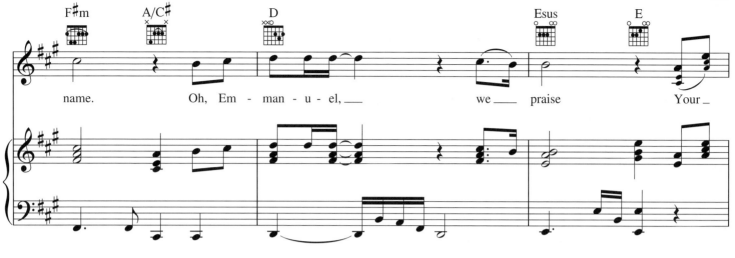

name. Oh, Em - man - u - el, ___ we ___ praise Your ___

name! _____

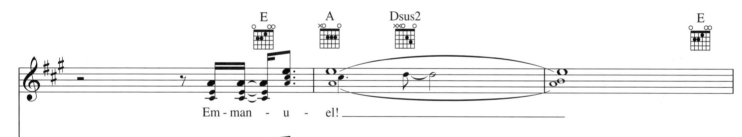

Em - man - u - el! _____

Re - joice!

THIS BABY

Words and Music by
STEVEN CURTIS CHAPMAN

teeth.
voice.

Al - most ev - 'ry - thing a - bout this lit - tle
There was the work to be done as a

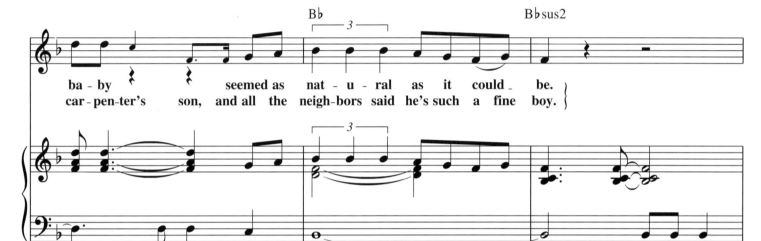

ba - by
car - pen-ter's son, and all the neigh-bors said he's such a fine boy.

But this {(1., D.S.) ba - by / boy —} made the an - gels sing, _____ and this {ba - by / boy —} made a

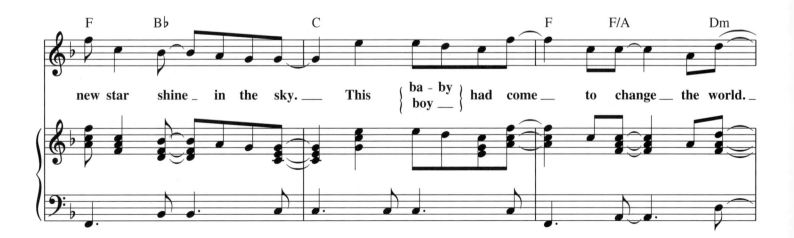

new star shine _ in the sky. __ This {ba - by / boy —} had come _ to change _ the world. _

This {ba - by / boy __} was God's __ own Son. _____

This {ba - by / boy __} was like __ no __ oth - er one. This {ba - by / boy __} was God __

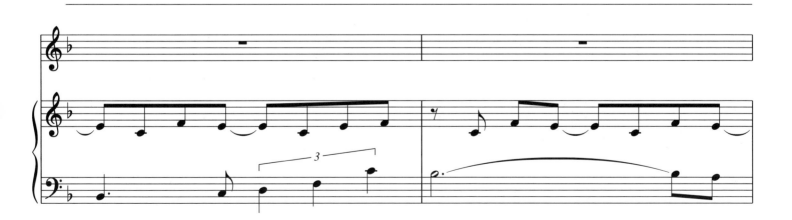

__ with us. _____ This ba - by was Je - sus. _____

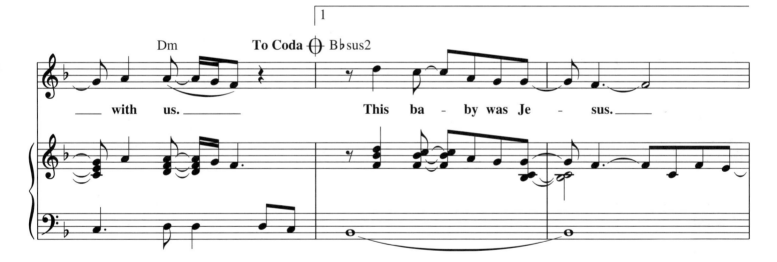

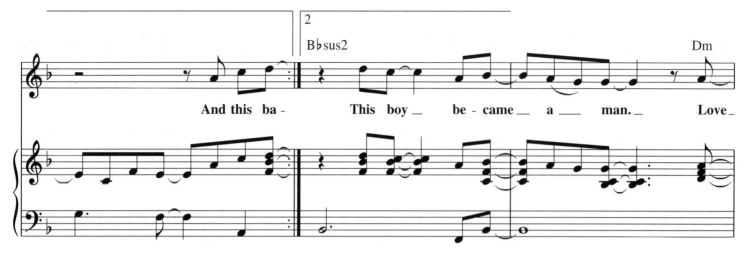

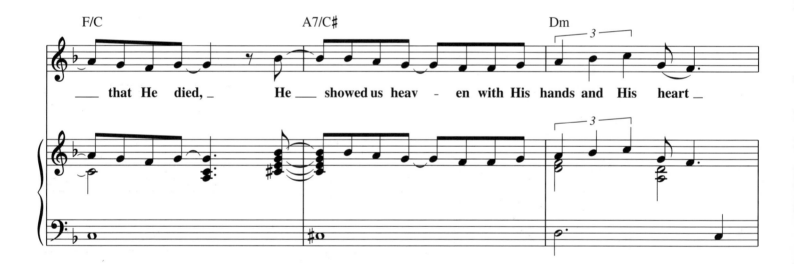

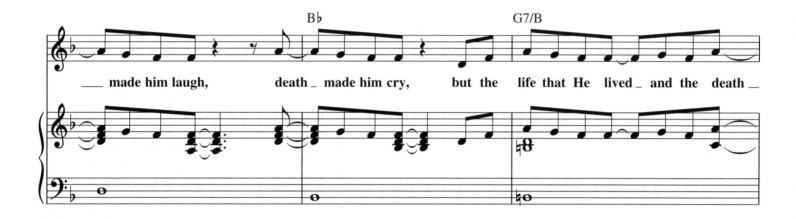

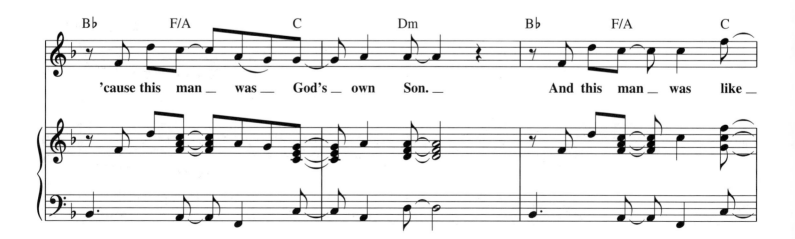

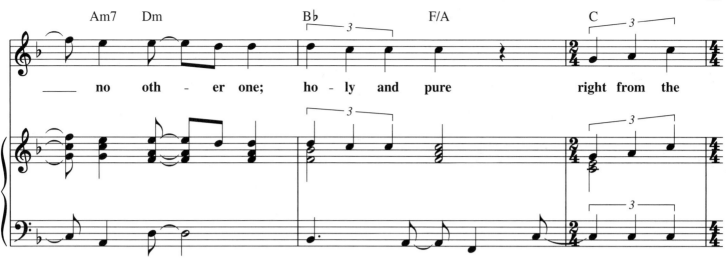

no oth - er one; ho - ly and pure right from the

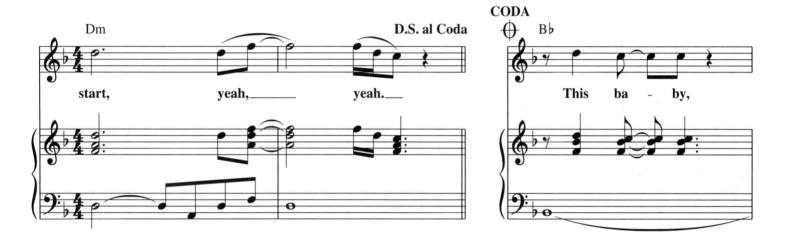

start, yeah,_____ yeah._____ This ba - by,

this ba - by was Je - sus._____

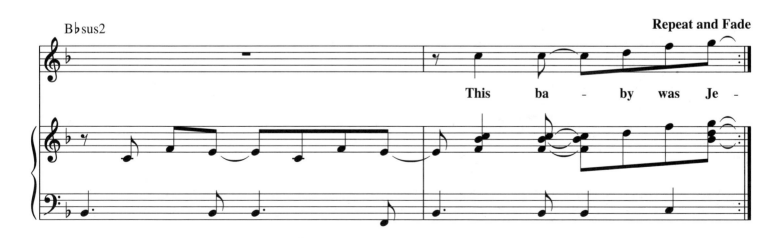

This ba - by was Je -

TO THE MYSTERY

Words and Music by
MICHAEL CARD

Driving, in 2

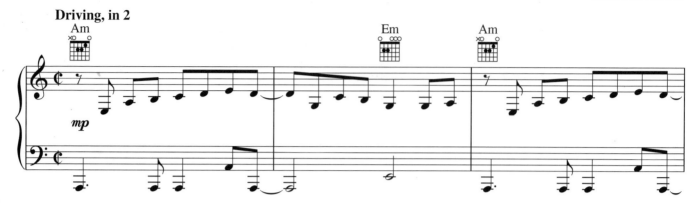

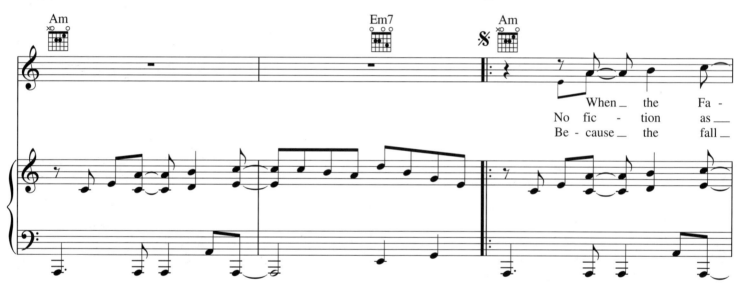

When _ the Fa -
No fic - tion as _
Be - cause _ the fall _

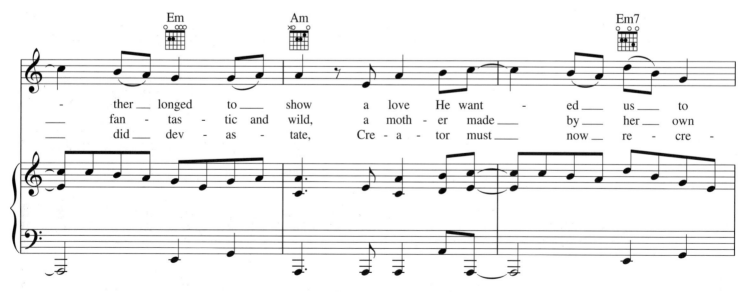

-ther _ longed to _ show a love He want - ed _ us to
_ fan - tas - tic and wild, a moth - er made _ by _ her own
_ did _ dev - as - tate, Cre - a - tor must _ now re - cre -

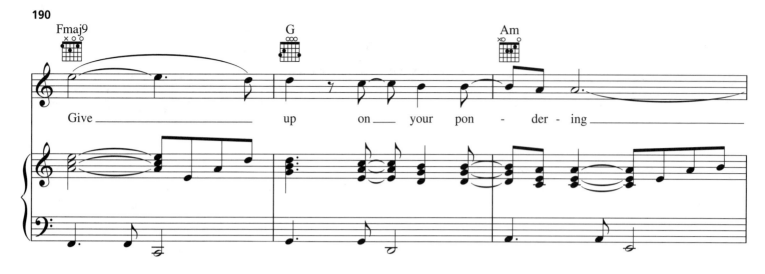

Give _____ up on ___ your pon - der - ing _____

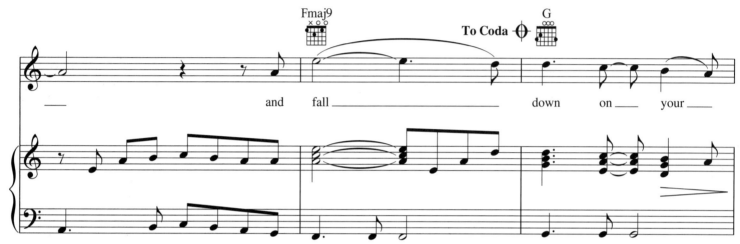

___ and fall _____ down on ___ your ___

1

knees! _____

2

knees! _____

Acoustic guitar solo

D.S. al Coda

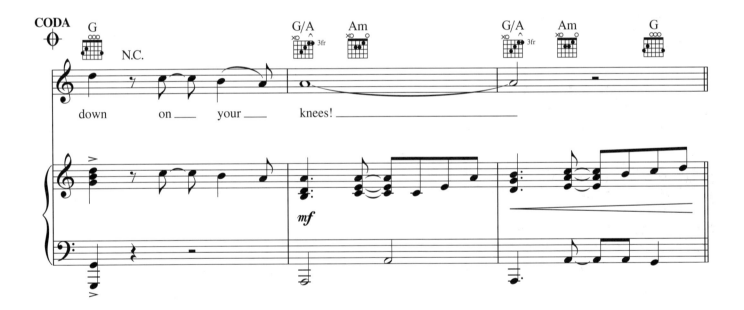

CODA

down   on ___   your ___   knees! _____

f *Flute solo*

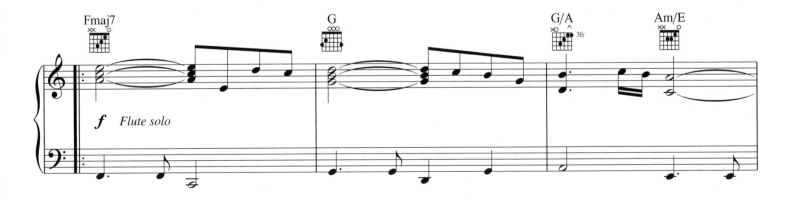

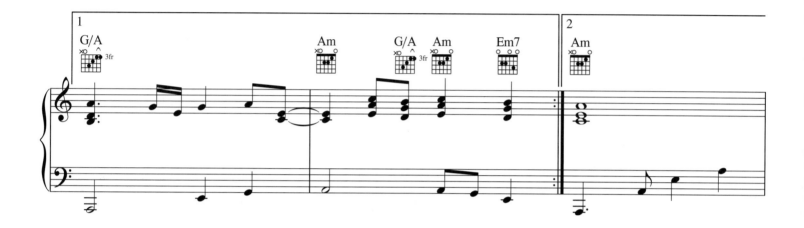

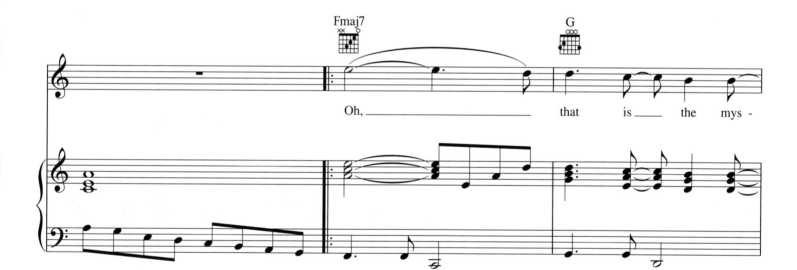

Oh, _____ that is ___ the mys-

- ter - y, _____ more _____

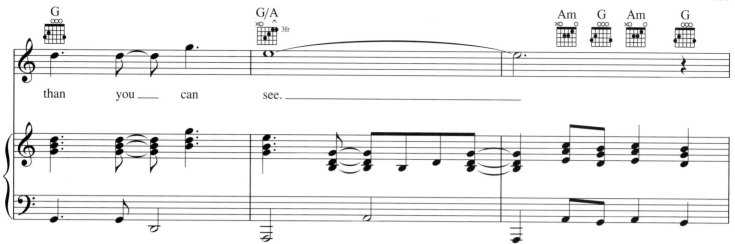

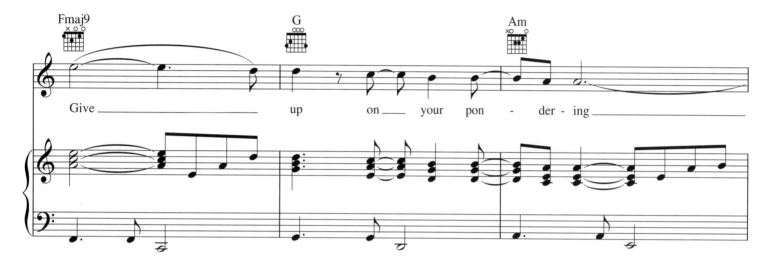

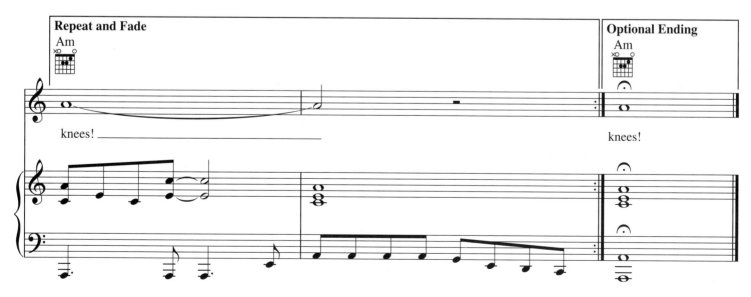

2000 DECEMBERS AGO

Words and Music by JOEL LINDSEY
and REGIE HAMM

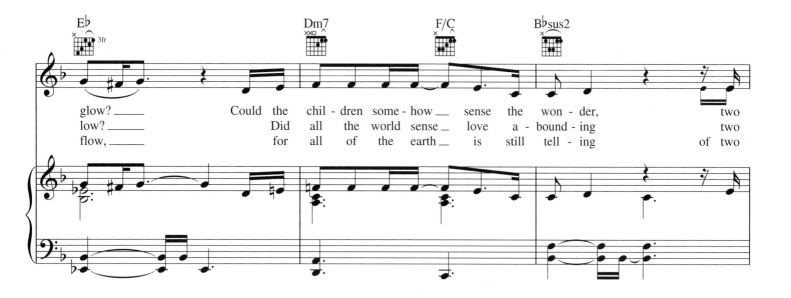

THE CHRISTIAN MUSICIAN

THE CHRISTIAN MUSICIAN series celebrates the many styles of music that make up the Christian faith. From Gospel favorites to today's hottest Christian artists, these books have something for all Christian musicians! There is no song duplication between any of the books!

CHRISTIAN ROCK

30 songs from today's hottest Contemporary Christian artists, including Audio Adrenaline, DC Talk, Delirious?, FFH, Jennifer Knapp, Jars of Clay, and Newsboys. Songs include: Consume Me • Everything • Flood • Get Down • Joy • One of These Days • Shine • Undo Me • and more.
00310953 Piano/Vocal/Guitar............$16.95

CLASSIC CONTEMPORARY CHRISTIAN

30 favorites essential to all Christian music repertoire, including: Arise, My Love • Awesome God • Friends • The Great Divide • His Strength Is Perfect • Love in Any Language • People Need the Lord • Where There Is Faith • and more.
00310954 Piano/Vocal/Guitar............$14.95

CLASSIC PRAISE & WORSHIP

Over 30 standards of the Praise & Worship movement, including: As the Deer • Great Is the Lord • He Is Exalted • Lord, I Lift Your Name on High • More Precious Than Silver • Oh Lord, You're Beautiful • Shine, Jesus, Shine • Step by Step • and more.
00310955 Piano/Vocal/Guitar............$14.95

CONTEMPORARY CHRISTIAN HITS

30 of today's top Christian favorites, from artists such as Avalon, Steven Curtis Chapman, DC Talk, MercyMe, Nichole Nordeman, Point of Grace, Rebecca St. James, ZOEgirl, and others. Songs include: Always Have, Always Will • Between You and Me • Can't Live a Day • Dive • Fool for You • God Is God • I Can Only Imagine • If This World • If You Want Me To • A Little More • Live Out Loud • My Will • Run to You • Steady On • Testify to Love • Wait for Me • and more.
00310952 Piano/Vocal/Guitar............$16.95

COUNTRY GOSPEL

Over 40 favorites, including: Church in the Wildwood • Crying in the Chapel • I Saw the Light • I Wouldn't Take Nothing for My Journey Now • Put Your Hand in the Hand • Turn Your Radio On • Will the Circle Be Unbroken • Wings of a Dove • and more.
00310961 Piano/Vocal/Guitar............$14.95

GOSPEL'S FINEST

Over 40 Gospel greats, including: Because He Lives • The Day He Wore My Crown • Great Is Thy Faithfulness • How Great Thou Art • In the Garden • More Than Wonderful • Precious Lord, Take My Hand • Soon and Very Soon • There's Something About That Name • and more.
00310959 Piano/Vocal/Guitar............$14.95

MODERN WORSHIP

Over 30 popular favorites of contemporary congregations, including: Above All • Ancient of Days • Breathe • The Heart of Worship • I Could Sing of Your Love Forever • It Is You • The Potter's Hand • Shout to the Lord • You Are My King (Amazing Love) • and more.
00310957 Piano/Vocal/Guitar............$14.95

SONGS FOR A CHRISTIAN WEDDING

35 songs suitable for services or receptions, including: Answered Prayer • Celebrate You • Doubly Good to You • Faithful Friend • Go There with You • Household of Faith • I Will Be Here • If You Could See What I See • My Place Is with You • Parent's Prayer (Let Go of Two) • Shine on Us • 'Til the End of Time • Where There Is Love • and more.
00310960 Piano/Vocal/Guitar............$16.95

SONGS OF FAITH FOR KIDS

50 favorites for kids of all ages! Includes: Arky, Arky • The B-I-B-L-E • Down in My Heart • God Is Bigger • He's Got the Whole World in His Hands • He's Still Workin' on Me • I'm in the Lord's Army • Lord, Be Glorified • Jesus Loves the Little Children • Salt and Light • This Little Light of Mine • Zacchaeus • and more.
00310958 Piano/Vocal/Guitar............$14.95

FOR MORE INFORMATION,
SEE YOUR LOCAL MUSIC DEALER,
OR WRITE TO:

HAL•LEONARD®
CORPORATION
7777 W. BLUEMOUND RD. P.O. BOX 13819
MILWAUKEE, WISCONSIN 53213

Visit Hal Leonard Online at
www.halleonard.com

Prices, contents, and availability subject to change without notice.